Gallipoli and Palestine 1915–18

ANZAC Soldier

VERSUS

Ottoman Soldier

Si Sheppard

Illustrated by Steve Noon

OSPREY PUBLISHING
Bloomsbury Publishing Plc
Kemp House, Chawley Park, Cumnor Hill, Oxford OX2 9PH, UK
29 Earlsfort Terrace, Dublin 2, Ireland
1385 Broadway, 5th Floor, New York, NY 10018, USA
E-mail: info@ospreypublishing.com
www.ospreypublishing.com

OSPREY is a trademark of Osprey Publishing Ltd

First published in Great Britain in 2023

A catalogue record for this book is available from the British Library.

ISBN: PB 9781472849182; eBook 9781472849199;
ePDF 9781472849168; XML 9781472849175

23 24 25 26 27   10 9 8 7 6 5 4 3 2 1

Maps by www.bounford.com
Index by Rob Munro
Typeset by PDQ Digital Media Solutions, Bungay, UK
Printed and bound in India by Replika Press Private Ltd.

FSC
MIX
Paper from
responsible sources
FSC® C016779
www.fsc.org

Osprey Publishing supports the Woodland Trust, the UK's leading
woodland conservation charity.

To find out more about our authors and books visit
www.ospreypublishing.com. Here you will find extracts, author
interviews, details of forthcoming events and the option to sign up for
our newsletter.

Author's dedication

Dedicated to New Zealand rugby; the heart and soul.

Ka mate, Ka mate
'Tis death, 'Tis death

Ka ora, Ka ora
'Tis life, 'Tis life

Artist's note

Readers may care to note that the original paintings from which the
colour plates in this book were prepared are available for private sale.
All reproduction copyright whatsoever is retained by the publishers.
All enquiries should be addressed to:

www.steve-noon.co.uk

The publishers regret that they can enter into no correspondence upon
this matter.

Key to military symbols

XXXXX Army Group	XXXX Army	XXX Corps	XX Division	X Brigade	III Regiment	II Battalion
I Company/Battery	••• Platoon	•• Section	• Squad	Infantry	Artillery	Cavalry
Airborne	Unit HQ	Air defence	Air Force	Air mobile	Air transportable	Amphibious
Anti-tank	Armour	Air aviation	Bridging	Engineer	Headquarters	Maintenance
Medical	Missile	Mountain	Navy	Nuclear, biological, chemical	Ordnance	Parachute
Reconnaissance	Signal	Supply	Transport movement	Fortress or static	MG Fortress machine gun	

Key to unit identification

Unit identifier — Commander — Parent unit
(+) with added elements
(–) less elements

CONTENTS

Introduction

Ottoman infantrymen with piled arms. These men are wearing the standard 1909 olive-drab field service uniform, complete with soft woollen cap, tunic, trousers, and puttees over half-boots, with a leather belt containing ammunition pouches, supported by a cross-belt over the chest. The figure on the left still has his knapsack on his back; this was a simplified version of the German M1887. Their neatly stacked Mauser rifles are German imports; Mauser variants (M1890, M1893 and M1903) were the standard Ottoman infantry rifle throughout World War I. Whereas the maelstrom of World War I would be a true baptism of fire for the overwhelming majority of young men serving with the Australian and New Zealand Army Corps (ANZAC), many of the rank and file in the Ottoman Army were veterans of combat in prior conflicts, and aware from an early age of the military heritage integral to their imperial identity. (Mondadori via Getty Images)

World War I – the Great War, the War to End all Wars – was a war of coalitions, a war of empires. In pursuit of strategic objectives they had no part in shaping, subject and colonial peoples from around the world were suddenly tasked with the obligation of shouldering arms at the behest of insular and exclusive policy-makers in far-off imperial capitals. Millions of men whose horizons had never before extended beyond their home towns or farms were thrust into combat of unprecedented intensity against counterparts with whom they had no previous quarrel; indeed, about whom they may only have had the haziest idea even existed.

Nowhere was this more explicit than in the confrontation between the British and Ottoman empires between 1914 and 1918, which would culminate in the utter dissolution of the centuries-old Ottoman imperial

ANZAC soldiers assemble in readiness for transfer from Egypt to the Dardanelles, 1915. In distinct contrast to the Ottoman Empire with its ancestral military traditions, Australia and New Zealand were young nations with fledgling military establishments. New Zealand infantry were fitted-out with the locally manufactured 1902 khaki pattern tunic. The Australian equivalent was based on the British model, but with roomier sleeves buttoned at the cuffs. Both armies were equipped with standard 1908 webbing set and the SMLE rifle. The largely neophyte Australian Imperial Force (AIF) and New Zealand Expeditionary Force (NZEF), originally embarked for the Western Front, were diverted to Egypt in late 1914. Reconstituted as the ANZAC under Lieutenant-General Sir William Riddell Birdwood, its units were first blooded in defence of the Suez Canal against an Ottoman raid in late January and early February 1915. (Universal History Archive/Universal Images Group via Getty Images)

hegemony and a fundamentally redrawn map of the entire Middle East, the unresolved legacy of which is critically relevant to this day. Committed to the existential challenge of total war, the British and Turkish hegemons at the cores of their respective empires increasingly drew upon their available reserves of manpower at the peripheries of their imperial orbits. Thus, Arabs, Kurds, Circassians and Turkmens serving in Ottoman uniform found themselves contesting battlefields trench by bloody trench with troops from Ireland, India, Nepal and, most distinctively, from the uttermost ends of the Earth: Australia and New Zealand.

Out of this maelstrom the national identities of three distinct contemporary states were forged. For Australia and New Zealand, this remains the ANZAC legend, born through sacrifice at Gallipoli; but it is just as relevant for the modern-day Republic of Turkey, defined by its founding father, Kemal Atatürk. His ascendancy began at that same bloody and desperate battle, against Antipodean antagonists he could never have imagined would be his nemesis just a year earlier, but with whose dogged and relentless pursuit he would still be grappling to the end of World War I.

The Ottoman Empire possessed a proud military heritage stretching back to its origins in the 14th century. By 1914, however, the empire was no longer rated as one of the great powers. Its failure to modernize had led to its economic marginalization and military obsolescence; generations of forced concessions to rival Russian and Western interests and the swelling nationalism of its subject peoples culminated in the humiliation of Ottoman defeat in the Balkan Wars of 1912–13. Anticipating this disaster, the reformists of the Committee of Union and Progress (CUP, *İttihad ve Terakki*), the so-called 'Young Turks', were increasingly assertive in directing official policy towards a fundamental reorganization of the empire. Reforming the Ottoman Army was a primary agenda of the CUP government that established one-party rule after seizing power in a coup (*Bâbıâli Baskını*) on 23 January 1913. Less than

Ottoman strategic objectives in World War I were ambiguous; in many ways, the empire was impelled into the conflict by forces beyond its control. Seized upon by the Young Turk faction as a means by which to consolidate their influence and advance their agenda of nationalism and modernization, the war effort evolved into an assertion of territorial integrity (against the British), internal sovereignty (against the Arab Revolt) and pan-Turanism expansion (against Russia).

Following the formal entry of the Ottoman Empire into World War I on 31 October 1914, the British planned a naval operation to force open passage of the Dardanelles; once Allied warships entered the Sea of Marmara they would have Constantinople at their mercy, compelling Sultan Mehmet V (r. 1909–18) to surrender. In the event, the attempt by Entente naval units on 18 March 1915 to penetrate the Narrows of the Dardanelles was a costly failure. Planning now shifted to a combined-arms amphibious operation, with Entente troops being landed on the coastline in order to neutralize Ottoman defences and clear the way for the ships. The landings would be conducted by

the Mediterranean Expeditionary Force (MEF), commanded by General Sir Ian Standish Monteith Hamilton, which incorporated the Australian and New Zealand Army Corps (ANZAC) alongside regular British and French units.

The beginning of 1916 would find the ANZACs back in Egypt, contesting with the Ottomans for control of the Sinai. On 10 March 1916 the Egyptian Expeditionary Force (EEF) was formed under the command of Lieutenant-General Sir Archibald James Murray. The Ottomans responded to the build-up of Allied troops at the logistical base of Romani by attacking it on 3 August 1916. Initial Ottoman success was brought to a halt by the New Zealand Mounted Rifles (NZMR) Brigade, whose defence of strategically critical Mount Royston checked the Ottoman advance and enabled an Allied counter-offensive that pushed the Ottomans out of their forward base at Katia on 5 August. This Allied success eliminated any future Ottoman threat to the Suez Canal and marked a shift in the strategic balance in the Middle East, where the Ottomans would thereafter be permanently on the defensive.

a month later, the Regulation for the General Organization of the Military (*Teşkilât-ı Umûmiye-i Askeriye Nizâmnâmesi*) was issued on 14 February. Urgency was emphasized when Enver Pasha replaced Ahmed İzzet Pasha as the Minister of War on 3 January 1914.

Although the Ottoman armed forces' lacklustre performance on the battlefield throughout the 19th and early 20th centuries had earned the Ottoman Empire the moniker 'The Sick Man of Europe', hundreds of thousands of its officers and men had recent experience of modern warfare in the Balkans, whereas the only previous combat experience their counterparts from Australia and New Zealand could possibly draw upon was as volunteers in the Second Anglo-Boer War (1899–1902). Australia had raised light-horse contingents to serve in that conflict, eventually sending 16,378 men. But for the overwhelming majority of both officers and rank and file of the fledgling Australian and New Zealand Army Corps (ANZAC), the Gallipoli campaign of 1915 would represent a steep learning curve.

The elite units of both dominions – the Australian Light Horse (ALH) and the New Zealand Mounted Rifles (NZMR) – were pioneering reflections of their respective frontier settler societies. Cavalry first appeared in the colonial militias formed in Australia from the mid-1850s onwards, and by 1885 all six colonies had mounted units. The first cavalry regiments formed in New Zealand appeared in 1863, with 21 mounted volunteer corps in existence by the 1870s. Unlike their infantry brethren, ALH troopers wore corded riding breeches, leather leggings bound by a spiral strap and leather equipment; during World War I they adopted a distinctive emu plume secured in the hat-band. NZMR troopers were outfitted similarly, with 1905 pattern leather equipment. (Fairfax Media via Getty Images via Getty Images)

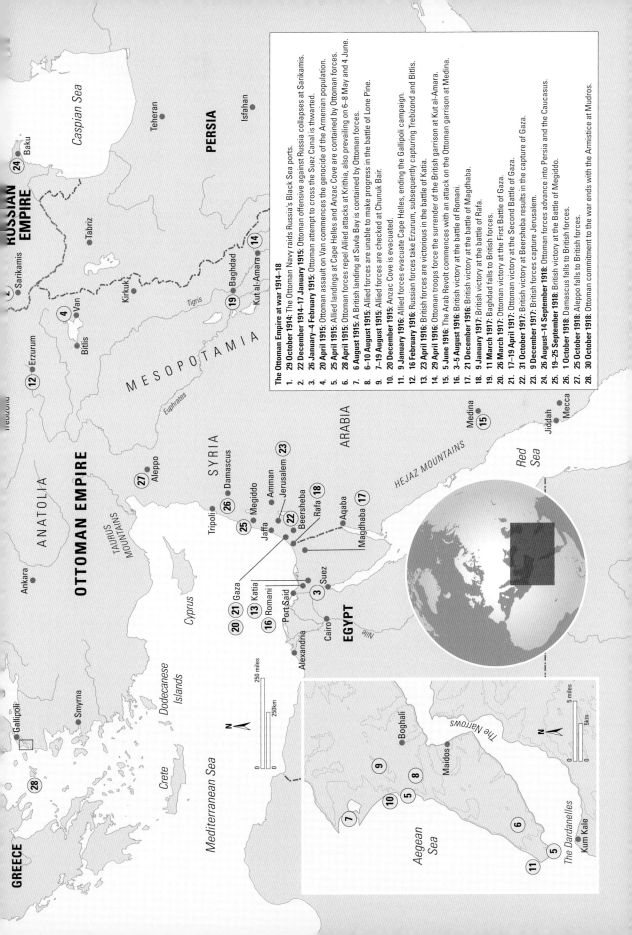

The Ottoman Empire at war 1914–18

1. **29 October 1914:** The Ottoman Navy raids Russia's Black Sea ports.
2. **22 December 1914–17 January 1915:** Ottoman offensive against Russia collapses at Sarikamis.
3. **January–4 February 1915:** Ottoman attempt to cross the Suez Canal is thwarted.
4. **20 April 1915:** Ottoman assault on Van commences the genocide of the Armenian population.
5. **25 April 1915:** Allied landings at Cape Helles and Anzac Cove are contained by Ottoman forces.
6. **28 April 1915:** Ottoman forces repel Allied attacks at Krithia, also prevailing on 6–8 May and 4 June.
7. **6 August 1915:** A British landing at Suvla Bay is contained by Ottoman forces.
8. **6–10 August 1915:** Allied forces are unable to make progress in the battle of Lone Pine.
9. **7–19 August 1915:** Allied forces are checked at Chunuk Bair.
10. **20 December 1915:** Anzac Cove is evacuated.
11. **9 January 1916:** Allied forces evacuate Cape Helles, ending the Gallipoli campaign.
12. **16 February 1916:** Russian forces take Erzurum, subsequently capturing Trebizond and Bitlis.
13. **23 April 1916:** British forces are victorious in the battle of Katia.
14. **29 April 1916:** Ottoman troops force the surrender of the British garrison at Kut al-Amara.
15. **5 June 1916:** The Arab Revolt commences with an attack on the Ottoman garrison at Medina.
16. **3–5 August 1916:** British victory at the battle of Romani.
17. **21 December 1916:** British victory at the battle of Magdhaba.
18. **9 January 1917:** British victory at the battle of Rafa.
19. **11 March 1917:** Baghdad falls to British forces.
20. **26 March 1917:** Ottoman victory at the First Battle of Gaza.
21. **17–19 April 1917:** Ottoman victory at the Second Battle of Gaza.
22. **31 October 1917:** British victory at Beersheba results in the capture of Gaza.
23. **9 December 1917:** British forces capture Jerusalem.
24. **26 August–14 September 1918:** Ottoman forces advance into Persia and the Caucasus.
25. **19–25 September 1918:** British victory at the Battle of Megiddo.
26. **1 October 1918:** Damascus falls to British forces.
27. **25 October 1918:** Aleppo falls to British forces.
28. **30 October 1918:** Ottoman commitment to the war ends with the Armistice at Mudros.

The Opposing Sides

Ottoman Army cadets. These young men were inducted into a military that was undergoing a rapid and forced transition. Responding to the catastrophe of defeat in the Turco-Italian War (1911–12) in Ottoman Tripolitania (modern-day Libya) and the Balkan Wars (1912–13), the new generation of 'Young Turks' who had risen to dominate the political establishment in Constantinople by 1914 dreamed of emulating the military doctrines of the German advisers upon whom they leaned by defeating their enemies in encirclement battles of annihilation (*kuşatma harekati*). In reality, the Ottoman Army's capacity for offensive action was extremely limited. Despite this, the stubborn courage of its rank and file and the professional initiative of its officer corps made the Ottoman Army, until its reserves of manpower were effectively exhausted in the last year of World War I, a redoubtable foe while on the defensive. (ullstein bild/ ullstein bild via Getty Images)

RECRUITMENT AND MOBILIZATION

Ottoman

According to the Army Act of 12 May 1914, the enlistment period was 25 years for the infantry, 20 for other arms and 17 for the Ottoman Navy, of which active service in regular forces (*Nizam*) was two, three and five years respectively. After this period of *Nizam* service, the men joined the reserve (*Redif*). When the Ottoman Empire declared mobilization on 3 August 1914, men born in 1891, 1892 and 1893 were already under arms. Men born during 1875–90 (i.e. aged 24–40) served in the active reserve (*ihtiyât*) of the *Redif*, while men born during 1868–74 (i.e. aged 40–45) served in the territorial reserve (*müstahfız*).

As reflected in this detachment of cavalry, the Ottoman Army, in many ways, appeared German. It was, in fact, modelled on the Imperial German Army, which had maintained a military mission in the Ottoman Empire since 1882. The Ottoman conscription and reserve system in use until late 1913 was patterned after the German model. The Ottoman General Staff was based on the German General Staff, as were the selection criteria and curriculum of the Ottoman War Academy. Moreover, the War Academy, as well as the tactical and branch schools of the Ottoman Army, used Imperial German Army manuals (translated into Ottoman Turkish) in its instruction. In addition, many influential Ottoman policy-makers, including Enver Pasha, had served as exchange officers in Germany. (ullstein bild/ullstein bild via Getty Images)

The Ottoman Army was 726,692 strong when mobilization was declared, increasing to 780,282 men by 25 September 1914. The total number of drafted men subsequently increased to 1,478,176 by March 1915, and reached 1,943,720 by 14 July 1915. By March 1916 it had reached 2,493,000 and by March 1917 2,855,000. These numbers do not include the irregular volunteers, such as Kurdish and Bedouin cavalry auxiliaries, who served alongside the Ottoman Army throughout World War I. Ultimately, the total number of men mobilized by the Ottoman Empire was close to 13 per cent of its overall population.

In reality, however, the response to the Ottoman call to arms was patchy. Military service was unpopular: conditions were harsh, leave was scarce and physical beatings were an endemic feature. Units in Yemen and the Hejaz (almost the entire Arabian Peninsula) were never mobilized, and the need for men on the part of the XI, XII and XIII corps, stationed respectively in eastern Anatolia, Mosul and Baghdad, could not be fulfilled due to widespread draft evasion and desertion. The pressure to make up shortfalls, already intense, only increased as World War I dragged on. The minimum draft age was lowered to 18 on 29 April 1915, and the maximum age for recruitment was increased to 50 on 20 March 1916.

The Ottoman armed forces entered World War I with many critical deficiencies. Although the Ottoman Constitution (*Kanûn-i Esâsî*) of 1876 declared that primary education was obligatory for every Ottoman subject, only one-fifth of Muslim children of school age actually attended primary schools in the academic year of 1913/14. The backbone of the Ottoman armed forces thus consisted overwhelmingly of illiterate peasants from the rural hinterland, who were physically tough but unsuited for a broad range of service in modern warfare.

Given the multi-ethnic basis of the Ottoman Empire, religion was a critical factor in recruitment and mobilization. On 11 November 1914, the highest religious authority in the empire, Şeyhülislam Ürgüplü Hayri Efendi, issued a

COMBAT Private, 14th Infantry Regiment

The Sari Bair offensive made good initial progress because the Ottoman high command had not anticipated concentrated enemy action being directed against the high ground; as Mustafa Kemal later bitterly commented, this was the decisive sector in the Ottoman defensive line, and the most inadequately defended. Until reinforcements could be rushed to their sector, those Ottoman units stationed on the slopes of Sari Bair – isolated detachments from the 19th, 5th and 16th divisions – bore the brunt of the assault alone. His patrol having stumbled upon an advance platoon of the enemy, both sides, shrouded by the pre-dawn darkness, being utterly unaware of the other's existence until the last moment, this infantryman has instinctively dropped into a crouch and launched himself into a charge.

Weapons, dress and equipment

Holding his Mauser M1890 bolt-action rifle (**1**) in an underhand grip, this soldier attacks with its attached M1890 bayonet (**2**).

He wears the German-style tunic (**3**) and breeches (**4**) with half-boots (**5**) adopted in 1909 in place of the old dark-blue uniform. Arm-of-service colours could be worn on the collar: infantry khaki, light infantry olive-green, artillery dark blue, cavalry light grey, engineers light blue, train red, general officers scarlet and staff officers crimson. Head-dress included the *burnous* for Arab units, but the regulation fez or fur tarboosh (*kalpac*) was usually replaced on active service by a distinctive greyish-khaki cloth helmet (**6**), styled a *kabalac* or *enverieh* ('Enver Pasha helmet').

The Ottoman soldier's individual combat kit normally included a leather belt with bayonet frog (**7**) and ammunition pouches holding 45 cartridges in three pockets that were exact copies of the German M1909. This man, however, has a locally manufactured alternative (**8**). Note how the rounds are exposed under the flaps of the pouches. While full combat kit included a rucksack that was a simplified version of the German M1887, this man has eschewed it in the heat of combat. He carries a canteen (**9**) that is a copy of the German *Feldflasche*.

religious decree (*fetvâ-yı şerîfe*) declaring holy war (*cihâd*). Throughout World War I, Ottoman propaganda emphasized military service was a binding religious duty (*farz-ı ayn*) with an emphasis on martyrdom (*şehâdet*). This was consequential for the empire's non-Muslim minorities. The Ottoman armed forces reflected the diverse nature of the empire. As a representative exemplar, the ethnic composition of the Yıldırım ('Lightning Bolt') Army Group was 66 per cent Turkish, 26 per cent Arab and 8 per cent others. Article 34 of the Temporary Law for Military Service, issued on 12 May 1914, divided military personnel into two categories: 'armed service' (*silahlı hizmet*) and 'unarmed service' (*silahsız hizmet*). The labour battalions of the latter were manned overwhelmingly by non-Muslim Ottoman enlisted men, primarily Armenians, Assyrians and Yezidis considered too untrustworthy to bear arms.

ANZAC

To replace its state-based militia system, Australia adopted national peacetime conscription for the first time in 1911. Men aged 18–25 were obliged to serve in the infantry militia for 16 days per year, including eight days in an annual camp, which provided the rudiments of military training. By 1914 the militia had about 51,200 men. There was no divisional structure, but officers gained some experience in command of units up to brigade level. The Defence Act of 1903 could not force existing militia members to serve overseas, however. Accordingly, the Australian Imperial Force (AIF) was brought into being on 15 August 1914. Initially a single division of 20,000 men under British command, by 1918 the AIF had grown to five divisions totalling more than 100,000 men, under Australian command.

In 1914, the inspector general of the Australian Army, Major-General William Throsby Bridges, believed no viable force could be derived from the militia units, as they were too recently established and what training they had

Friends and families bid farewell to departing troops of the AIF, Sydney. Australia attempted to introduce conscription twice during World War I, first in 1916 and then in 1917. In the two referenda that were held to decide the issue, however, Australian voters rejected conscription on both occasions. Australia thus retained a volunteer army through to the end of World War I, the only belligerent country to do so. Ultimately, 416,809 men enlisted, from a total population of fewer than 5 million. (Fairfax Media via Getty Images via Getty Images)

NZEF soldiers from Taranaki, 1915. At the outbreak of World War I, a heavy emphasis was placed on ANZAC recruitment of officers and men from the same state (Australia) or province (New Zealand), ideally from the same region; units were intended to be local and territorial to enhance loyalty and attachment. The AIF recruits serving with the Australian 1st Division were organized on a territorial basis, with the 1st Brigade (1st–4th battalions) consisting of men from New South Wales, the 2nd Brigade (5th–8th battalions) consisting of men from Victoria and the 3rd Brigade (9th–12th battalions) from the other states and territories. As the war evolved and the pool of available manpower necessary for the creation of units with a specific geographic focus began to dry up, the emphasis shifted towards the creation of units with a more 'national' identity. For example, the battalions and companies of the New Zealand Rifle Brigade, which was established in April 1915 as a second New Zealand infantry brigade to complement the brigade then serving at Gallipoli, were assigned numerical designations as opposed to provincial identities. (Hulton Archive/ Getty Images)

was based on home defence. Nevertheless, of the 20,000 original volunteers who joined the AIF, 26 per cent were militia members, a disproportionately large number of whom provided the initial pool for junior and non-commissioned officers. The great bulk of the remaining volunteers had either no military service (42 per cent) or were former state militia members.

In New Zealand, the Defence Act of 1909 made military training compulsory for all men aged 18–25, followed by five years of service in the reserve. At the outbreak of World War I, quotas were easily surpassed, as volunteers flocked to enlist in the New Zealand Expeditionary Force (NZEF), 52,561 being accepted by December 1914. Such was the clamour for combat that many New Zealand teenagers officially too young to fight resorted to subterfuge in order to serve in uniform. At the other end of the scale, Arthur Richard Fitzherbert, born in England on 9 November 1853, was more than 20 years over the cut-off age for enlistment, but managed to pass himself off as a man of 40 and served with the New Zealand Mounted Rifles (NZMR) Brigade in Egypt alongside his eldest son, Arthur Jr. On 27 March 1917, aged 63 years old, Trooper Fitzherbert of the Wellington Mounted Rifles died of wounds received in action the previous day, during the First Battle of Gaza.

As the number of New Zealand volunteers began to dry up, however, increasingly coercive measures were introduced to encourage enlistment. From November 1915, men of military age were banned from leaving New Zealand without the government's permission. From February 1916, men who had enlisted for, or been discharged or exempted from, military service were required to wear armbands in public to distinguish them from 'shirkers' who had yet to enlist. Conscription finally arrived in New Zealand with the Military Service Act in August 1916. This empowered the government to call up any man aged 20–45 for military service at home or abroad. Conscription initially applied to single men without wives or children, but was extended to men who were married but childless in October 1917. By the end of

Among the units committed to the Sari Bair offensive was the New Zealand Native Contingent (NZNC), which had landed at Gallipoli on 3 July 1915, composed of 16 officers with 461 rank and file, representative of the indigenous Māori population of Aotearoa/New Zealand. The Māori would acquit themselves bravely, but at great cost, over the course of the 6–10 August offensive, losing 17 men killed, 89 wounded and two missing. Jumping off at night, the offensive was enabled to make initial progress by the cover of darkness, but it also led to disorientation and fragmentation among the attacking columns, which became separated as they clambered uphill into rough terrain. In this environment, combat devolved into isolated individual actions as opposing forces blundered into each other. This young man has been caught up in just such an encounter, his platoon being surprised by an Ottoman patrol.

Weapons, dress and equipment

Surprised by the sudden onrush of his antagonist at close quarters, this man has instinctively dropped into the traditional fighting stance of a Māori warrior, wielding his Short Magazine Lee-Enfield No. 1 Mk III bolt-action rifle (**1**) in the style of a *taiaha*, the ancestral Māori war club staff weapon.

The 1909 London Imperial Conference had advocated for standardization across the military forces of the British Empire, so the ANZACs were dressed, equipped and armed similarly to their British counterparts. New Zealand troops wore a thick woollen khaki uniform (**2**) and leather boots (**3**) similar to their counterparts in the Australian Imperial Force (AIF). The main distinction between the ANZACs was their choice of headgear. While the Australians could be identified by their signature broad-brimmed slouch hat with a rising-sun badge, the New Zealanders at Gallipoli typically sported a cap (**4**) that would only be superseded by the distinctive 'lemon-squeezer'-style hat subsequent to the campaign. Like this

man, many New Zealanders improvised canvas flaps (**5**) to protect the backs of their necks from the fierce summer sun. His cap badge (**6**) incorporates two traditional Māori weapons, the *taiaha* and *tewhatewha*, crossed through a crown. Its motto reads 'Te Hokowhitu a Tū' ('the seventy twice-told warriors of the war god'), signifying the 140 warriors of the Māori war god, Tū-mata-uenga. His NZNC title badge (**7**) is featured on his left shoulder. He wears the simple white cloth armbands (**8**) issued for this operation, intended as visual markers to help with unit cohesion.

This man carries the standard set of woven-cotton Pattern 1908 webbing, incorporating ten cartridge pouches (**9**) – sufficient for 150 rounds of ammunition. His gear includes a bayonet frog for his Pattern 1907 bayonet (**10**), a water bottle with holder (**11**), an entrenching tool with holder (**12**) and a haversack (**13**), here worn on the left hip but frequently worn on the back; he has removed his backpack as an unnecessary encumbrance in combat.

World War I, 98,850 men from New Zealand – 79,302 volunteers and 19,548 conscripts – had served king and country overseas, from a pool of approximately 250,000 men of eligible age in 1914, or 9.1 per cent of New Zealand's total population.

LEADERSHIP AND ORGANIZATION

Ottoman

The CUP appreciated that modernization of the Ottoman Army would require foreign tutoring. Accordingly, in a decision ripe with geopolitical significance, the Ottoman Empire concluded an agreement with Berlin on 27 October 1913. Contracted for five years with the option of an extension, a German military mission under the leadership of Generalleutnant Otto Liman von Sanders arrived in Constantinople on 14 December to assist with the reform process. The German advisers would play a significant role not just in the development but also in the deployment of the Ottoman Army.

Upon becoming Minister of War in January 1914, one of Enver Pasha's first initiatives was to retire approximately 1,300 elderly high-ranking Ottoman Army officers, scapegoated for defeat in the Balkan Wars and regarded as an obstruction to the modernization effort. They were replaced by a new class of younger officers, whose primary qualification was loyalty to the CUP. Though defined by a political narrative, it was this next generation who would emerge as the backbone of the Ottoman war effort and subsequently as the founders of the modern Turkish republic.

In August 1914, the Ottoman military establishment was composed of four field army commands – the First Army in Constantinople, the Second Army in Edirne, the Third Army in Erzincan and the Fourth Army in Damascus, each of which commanded three army corps – plus an independent army corps in Yemen and two independent divisions in Asir (north of Yemen) and the Hejaz respectively. In addition, two regions (the Bosporus and Dardanelles Straits) and two cities (Edirne and Erzurum) that had been designated fortified zones were placed under the control of the fortress artillery inspectorate-general.

When the Ottoman Empire entered World War I, Oberst Friedrich Bronsart von Schellendorf quickly became the de facto Chief of the Ottoman General Staff, which he immediately began reorganizing along the lines of its German equivalent. In the process, Liman assumed command of the First Army, with responsibility for the defence of Thrace, including Constantinople. He held this position until 24 March 1915, when he was assigned command of the new Fifth Army, dedicated to the defence of the Dardanelles, while Generalfeldmarschall Colmar von der Goltz succeeded him in command of the First Army. The Fifth Army was the first of several new establishments as the Ottoman Army continued to expand over the course of the war. The Sixth Army was activated on 5 September 1915; the Seventh Army on 12 August 1917; the Eighth Army on 2 October 1917; and the Ninth Army on 7 June 1918. Reflecting the evolving geopolitical environment, in order to take advantage of collapse of authority in post-Tsarist Russia and fulfil Enver Pasha's dream of pan-Turanism, the Islamic Army of the Caucasus

(in reality only a corps-sized formation including Caucasian volunteers) was activated on 10 July 1918. In conjunction with the Ninth Army – and at cross purposes with its German ally – this unit went on the offensive in Persia and the Caucasus, taking Tabriz on 23 August, Baku on 15 September and Derbent on 7 October.

The pervasive German influence at the top of the Ottoman command structure reflected the consensus that the crash modernization programme undertaken in the wake of the disastrous Balkan and Libyan defeats was still a work in progress and the empire was not yet ready to fight a major war against any of the great powers. While the mobilized personnel strength of the Ottoman military was imposing – more than 1 million men, with a combat strength of 820,000 – just 12,469 of this total were of officer rank, a ratio of only 1.5 officers for every 100 combat soldiers. The Ottoman military did not have a reserve officer system or a professional NCO corps. Almost all NCOs acquired their skills and learnt their trade through practical experience in units and on campaign without any systematic or organized training. Finding volunteers for this ad hoc method of organic self-promotion through the ranks was a perennial problem due in large part to the low salary and the insecure tenure of NCOs.

Upon mobilization, military-academy cadets were immediately assigned to units as brevet lieutenants (*zabit vekili*), while senior students of the military secondary schools and civilian high-school graduates were inducted as officer candidates (*zabit namzeti*). Officer-training courses (*zabit talimgâhları*) were opened for new cadets, who graduated after 6–8 months and were sent to the front with the rank of corporal. After such men had served a six-month probation as NCOs, unit commanders could decide to commission them as officers. The Ottoman Empire's high schools had enough graduates to fill the necessary quotas for only one year, however. After 1915 the high command resorted to enrolling graduates from the religious schools (*medrese*), and ultimately every available untapped source was used in order to overcome mounting casualty figures. This opened the door to meritocratic promotion, so that by the end of the war Arabs represented around 15 per cent of the total officer corps.

ANZAC

As New Zealand, with a total population of little more than 1 million, did not yet have sufficient men to form its own division, and Australia did not have quite enough men at first to form a second division, the Australian 4th Brigade and the New Zealand Infantry Brigade were merged into a joint New Zealand and Australian Division. In preparation for the 1915 Gallipoli campaign, the AIF and the NZEF were merged to create the ANZAC, commanded by the British Army's Major-General William Riddell Birdwood.

While there was no shortage of volunteers flocking to the colours, finding qualified officers to command the newly created units was more problematic. Senior officers, ideally veterans of the fighting in South Africa, were available, but the junior officer ranks were very green in terms of staff qualifications as well as combat experience. In contrast to the old militia policy in New Zealand of electing officers, it was only subsequent to the Imperial Conference of 1909 that officer candidates for both the Staff Corps and the Territorial Force had to follow the British Army model of passing entrance examinations for commissions. With only a small professional military force, New Zealand could not justify establishing its own military academy, so candidates who applied for regular commissions in the Staff Corps were required to attend an intensive three-year officer cadet course at the Royal Military College of Australia at Duntroon. This had the positive effect of homogenizing military doctrine between the two dominions at the highest level. An interchange system was also introduced that saw Imperial officers seconded to the Australian and New Zealand Staff Corps, while a number of officers from the dominions attended courses and were attached to regiments in Britain. Significantly, prior to service overseas with the NZEF, all non-commissioned officers were required to complete a five-week course at Trentham Army Camp identical to that of the officers. This would pay dividends as the war unfolded, as most NCOs who survived the early campaigns would go on to receive commissions to replace heavy combat officer casualties, especially within the infantry battalions.

Initially, the ANZAC consisted of the Australian 1st Division, under Major-General Bridges; the New Zealand and Australian Division, under Major-General Alexander John Godley; and two mounted brigades – the Australian 1st Light Horse Brigade and the NZMR Brigade. During the Gallipoli campaign, reinforcements formed an Australian 2nd Division on 10 July 1915; commanded by Major-General James Gordon Legge, this arrived in time for the ill-fated August offensives. The ANZAC returned to Egypt from Gallipoli in December 1915, when a further influx of volunteers allowed the AIF to expand significantly. On 2 February 1916 the 3rd Division was created, and officers and NCOs from the 1st Division provided leadership cadres around which the 4th and 5th divisions were subsequently raised. In February 1916 the ANZAC was reorganized into I and II ANZAC corps, which saw service on the Western Front until being further reorganized in November 1917, all five Australian infantry divisions being concentrated into the Australian Corps, while the New Zealand Division was subsumed into the British XXII Corps.

In March 1916 the ANZAC Mounted Division was formed in Egypt, commanded by Australian Major-General Henry George 'Harry' Chauvel. To

spearhead the Allied struggle for the Sinai, in December 1916 the Mounted Division was combined with the British 42nd and 52nd Infantry divisions and the Imperial Camel Corps Brigade to form the Desert Column, commanded by British Lieutenant-General Sir Philip Walhouse Chetwode. In April 1917 Chauvel, now a lieutenant-general, succeeded to command of the Desert Column, command of the Mounted Division devolving to New Zealand Major-General Edward Walter Clervaux Chaytor. The Desert Column was expanded into a full Desert Mounted Corps in August 1917, incorporating the ANZAC Mounted Division with 1st and 2nd ALH brigades, NZMR Brigade and British 22nd Yeomanry Mounted Rifles Brigade; the Australian Mounted Division, with 3rd and 4th ALH brigades and the Yeomanry units of the British 5th and 6th Mounted brigades and XIX Brigade, Royal Horse Artillery; and the Imperial Camel Corps Brigade.

LOGISTICS AND MORALE

Ottoman

While the Ottoman mobilization effort was a significant achievement, the capacity of the Ottoman Empire, which remained critically under-industrialized in 1914, to equip this available pool of manpower properly was a separate question. Despite the imposition of war taxes (*tekâlif-i harbiye*) incorporating draconian measures that authorized the confiscation of any *matériel* considered vital to the war effort from the civilian sector at prices determined by the state, meeting the logistical needs of the military remained a major challenge for the Ottoman authorities throughout World War I. This was evident from the beginning, when the mobilization order required that each conscript bring staples such as bread, dried foods and sugar sufficient to feed himself for five days. Enlisted men were also required to bring their own uniforms (or at least appropriate clothes that could serve the function of uniforms) and good shoes. According to a report by the commander of the 17th Division in the III Corps Zone, more than half of the troops were still wearing civilian clothes even as late as mid-1915.

RIGHT
Sacrificing goats, an Ottoman pre-battle ritual, 1915. Official emphasis of the religious aspects of the struggle helped bolster the commitment of the rank and file to faith-based military traditions such as martyrdom and the status of holy warrior (*gâzilik*). Routine religious obligations were observed in the military, even during combat, and there were established posts within the units, such as battalion prayer leaders (*tabur imamlari*), who worked to maintain troop morale throughout World War I. (Underwood Archives/Getty Images)

FAR RIGHT
The Ottoman Army had to fight in a wide range of environments, most of them lacking secure, reliable communications and transport networks. Here, supplies for the front in Mesopotamia are unloaded from the uncompleted Baghdad railway and transferred to mules in the mountainous area of Kurdistan. Conversely, in the Dardanelles, Ottoman forces would benefit from the possession of interior lines with their commensurate ease of communication and supply. The Ottoman rank and file serving at Gallipoli were allocated 3,149 calories in rations per day and enjoyed a reasonably varied diet including 900g of bread each day and fresh fruit and vegetables when they were in season. Critically, they enjoyed the inestimable advantage of access to abundant sources of fresh water. Moreover, on a periodic basis units were pulled out of the front line and rotated back to rest camps safely out of enemy artillery fire range. (ullstein bild/ullstein bild via Getty Images)

From the moment hostilities commenced, the Ottoman Empire's armed forces remained almost entirely dependent on its German ally to meet its needs for everything from small arms to artillery guns. This was problematic, for wartime blockades meant that the Ottoman Empire was cut off from its sole source of support. The situation persisted throughout the Gallipoli campaign, only improving when Bulgaria entered the conflict on the side of the Central Powers in October 1915. The invasion and conquest of Serbia a month later opened a direct land route to Germany and restored the Ottoman Empire's access to German arms and munitions. Over the course of World War I, Germany contributed 559 heavy guns, 500,000 artillery shells, 557,000 rifles, 930 million rifle cartridges, 1,600 machine guns, 300 aircraft, 16,000 gas masks and 30 flame-throwers to the Ottoman cause.

Whereas at Gallipoli the Ottoman fighting men had every advantage, in the Middle East that paradigm shifted completely, as the limited capacity of the Ottoman Empire to meet the needs of its expanding military became increasingly salient. Simply put, even with German support, Ottoman policy-makers would be unable to coax enough output from an already inadequate manufacturing base through an over-stressed supply chain to where it was desperately needed. In a report on the general military situation on 20 September 1917, Mustafa Kemal pointed out that the available personnel of many corps in his Seventh Army was only one-fifth of what was actually needed, while those actually in uniform were either veterans debilitated by disease or untrained draftees aged 17–20 or 45–55.

The situation only worsened in 1918. The average daily ration of the Ottoman soldier on the Palestine front in March 1918 was only 500–600g of bread, with a little wheat porridge and perhaps a few vegetables. By September 1918 rations had declined further to 125g of bread and boiled beans in the morning, at noon and at night, without oil or any other condiment. Ottoman soldiers in Palestine had been reduced to eating the husks of oats and barley in lieu of the grain itself. This dire subsistence-level crisis also applied to fodder, and the ensuing lack of cavalry mounts and pack animals severely compromised mobility. A corresponding problem was the struggle to keep the Ottoman forces properly clothed and shod. Liman complained in 1918 that the clothing of the troops was so bad that many officers under his command wore ragged uniforms, and even some battalion commanders had to wear rawhide sandals (*çarık*) instead of boots.

ANZAC

An equally disinterested attitude towards parade-ground discipline prevailed throughout the ANZAC ranks during World War I. This was clearly evident at Gallipoli, where idiosyncratic improvisation and displays of initiative in terms of uniforms and weapons were tolerated if not actively encouraged. At Gallipoli, where deployment meant no relief from service on the front line, such behaviour did not impinge upon combat effectiveness. In other sectors, however, that attitude could be problematic, and the AIF rapidly garnered a reputation for 'larrikin' behaviour. Even amongst the Dominion contingents, the Australians were far more likely to be behind bars (nine prisoners per 1,000 troops) than the Canadians, New Zealanders, or South Africans (1.6 prisoners per 1,000 troops). A total of 129 Australians were sentenced to death over the course of World War I, mainly for desertion, but none was actually executed. Section 98 of the 1903 Australian Commonwealth Defence Act stated that all death sentences had to be counter-signed by the Australian Governor General, and this never happened. New Zealand troops had a better reputation generally, but were also responsible for the worst ANZAC atrocity while posted overseas, the massacre of the male inhabitants of the Arab village of Surafend on 10 December 1918 in retaliation for the murder of an NZMR Brigade trooper. Significantly, the perpetrators were never identified; whether conscript or volunteers, the culture of ANZAC 'mateship' created a strong bond of camaraderie.

This bond, forged at Gallipoli, was critical to maintaining the high standards of combat performance that made ANZAC mounted units the shock troops of British operations throughout subsequent campaigns. After the cramped beachheads of Gallipoli, which afforded no room to deploy, let alone utilize, men on horseback, the subsequent ANZAC commitment to the Middle East at least allowed space for effective cavalry action. The deserts of the Sinai and southern Palestine were no paradise, however. The sand was ubiquitous, clogging everything from food to the mechanisms of rifles. Temperatures could reach 54°C, and even higher when the *khamsin*, a hot desert wind that blew across the Sinai, whipped up sandstorms. On one occasion, a reconnaissance by the 6th ALH Regiment to Bir el-Bayud had to be called off when the heat became unbearable. Four officers and 32 men were evacuated to hospital suffering from sunstroke, and nearly all of the regiment's 500 horses were unfit for duty, requiring three days to recover. A grim reality of such conditions was that decomposition occurred

FAR LEFT
An Australian soldier lies wounded in the foreground, as hundreds of other soldiers move among the dead and wounded on the beach at Anzac Cove on the day of the landing, 25 April 1915. Although subsequently better organized, the inherent vulnerability of the cramped beachhead, the indispensable lifeline for the entire operation, is apparent; had the Ottomans possessed sufficient artillery they could have rendered Anzac Cove unviable and forced its evacuation months in advance of the actual timeframe. (Philip Schuller/The AGE/ Fairfax Media via Getty Images via Getty Images)

LEFT
ANZAC troops landing supplies near Gaba Tepe, April/May 1915. In contrast to their Ottoman opponents at Gallipoli, ANZAC and other Allied forces, clinging to two tiny beachheads, would depend absolutely on supply routes stretching across the Mediterranean Sea to the port city of Alexandria in Egypt. While their Ottoman rivals enjoyed access to open country, fresh food and running water, the ANZACs were penned into a confined space with rudimentary sanitation and had their subsistence needs entirely met by canned goods and water either delivered in containers from the Greek islands or eked out of desperate improvisation with condensers and hastily dug wells. (Hulton Archive/Getty Images)

rapidly, with bodies becoming bloated and turning black after only two hours in the sun.

In this environment, the limit of combat operations was defined by access to water. At Romani, troopers of the 1st ALH Regiment had to survive on the contents of their water bottles alone for 35 hours. The regiment's horses were not watered at all for 56 hours. Control over the sources of water thus defined not just tactical operations but grand strategy, epitomized at Beersheba on 31 October 1917, when the entire contest for mastery of the Middle East devolved upon whether ANZACs or Ottomans could claim the town's wells by nightfall.

WEAPONS, TRAINING AND TACTICS

Ottoman

The standard Ottoman infantry weapon was the 7.65mm Mauser M1903 bolt-action rifle, a German weapon with a five-round removable box magazine and a 600m effective range; just over 200,000 were received by the Ottoman armed forces before World War I. Previous versions of the Mauser design – the 7.65mm Mauser M1890 and M1893 bolt-action rifles – were also in Ottoman service. Obsolete weapons such as the 9.5mm Mauser M1887 rifle and the 11.43mm Peabody-Martini M1874 single-shot rifle were issued to second-line units, Kurdish and Arab auxiliaries and the paramilitary Jardama. The standard handguns used by officers were the 7.63mm Mauser C/96 and 9mm FN-Browning M1903. In addition to manufacturing the MG 08 – the 7.92mm version of the British-designed Maxim medium machine gun – for the Imperial German Army, Deutsche Waffen- und Munitionsfabriken also produced a 7.65mm export version, the MG 09, which was sold to Bulgaria, China, Romania and the Ottoman Empire. Both weapons had an effective range of 2,000m and fired at a rate of 300rd/min.

Under the influence of the Young Turks, the Ottoman state had emerged as a trend-setter in military doctrine. In 1911, the standard square infantry division of the Ottoman Army, composed of two brigades of two infantry regiments each, was revised to a triangular division of three infantry regiments. Under this arrangement the number of infantry battalions in an infantry division was reduced from 16 to nine. This proved a remarkably prescient

Some aspects of Ottoman Army training reflected the close-order combat formations of an earlier age, as indicated by this photograph published in 1914. Prior to World War I, advocates of an open-order approach to combat recommended a decentralization of infantry tactics. Traditionalists scoffed at the so-called democratization of the battlefield, however, fearing it would lead to a loss of discipline and command and control. They emphasized that offensive operations should continue to uphold the established military principle of concentration of overwhelming power at the decisive point. As an alternative to the free-form, open-order tactics advocated by the reformists, traditionalists proposed pushing attacking infantry forward in short bounds of small, mutually supporting line formations, firing as they advanced. (Culture Club/ Getty Images)

An Ottoman artillery crew in the Suez Canal sector, January 1915. The Ottoman attempt to storm the canal, during which Ottoman and ANZAC troops clashed for the first time, was intended to degrade British imperial authority by closing the canal to Allied shipping and inspiring a pan-Islamic revolt in Egypt. Each Ottoman infantry division was supposed to be supported by six batteries of field guns, but in reality they had to make do with three or four at most. The most common types of Ottoman field artillery during World War I were German-designed and manufactured 7.5cm and 7.7cm field guns. The 7.5cm Krupp M03 L/30 field gun had a range of 6,000m; 648 were purchased from Germany in the period before World War I, although many were lost in the Balkan Wars. After 1916 Germany supplied its Ottoman allies with both types of the standard German Army field gun: the 7.7cm Krupp M96 L/27 nA (range 7,800m) and the 7.7cm Rheinmetall M16 L/35 (range 9,000m). Desperately short of field artillery, the Ottoman Army also used many older and obsolescent field guns, some dating back to the 1870s, as well as captured Russian and British guns. The latter were of a different calibre to the German guns and could be used only while stocks of captured artillery shells lasted. (ullstein bild/ullstein bild via Getty Images)

decision, for in the static trench-warfare environment of World War I the large four-regiment infantry division proved to be unwieldy and organizationally unsuited to tactical requirements. The Ottoman model enabled an infantry division to maintain two regiments in contact with the enemy and one regiment in reserve, which proved an ideal organizational solution to the tactical requirements of trench warfare. The Imperial German Army would be the first European army to begin converting its four-regiment divisions to the Ottoman model in 1915, one adopted by every major combatant European army by 1918.

Ottoman tactical doctrine was heavily influenced by German military thinking, which, by the early 20th century, was itself undergoing a process of evolution away from the old standards of 'Prussian Drill' that had proved so successful in the conflicts against the Hapsburg Empire in 1866 and France in 1870–71. Observing how the British had struggled to apply linear tactics against modern firepower during the Second Anglo-Boer War, some German General Staff officers suggested reforms, known as 'Boer Tactics', whereby non-commissioned officer-led squads would advance dispersed and irregularly taking advantage of available cover. The Germans did revise their drill regulations in 1906 to conform to lessons learnt from recent wars, but the changes left close control and the old 'Prussian Drill' standard intact. While advising commanders to deploy columns into skirmish lines if crossing fire-swept ground, the regulations warned that surrendering close-order formation was undesirable and often avoidable if the skirmish line could approach close enough to the enemy line to weaken its fire. Officers were urged to deploy skirmish lines in depth whenever possible. The established belief that only close control made possible fire and movement meant that once the skirmishers reached medium range and opened fire the advance would have to proceed in platoon-strength rushes; the 'Boer Tactics' approach of advancing by squads was criticized for slowing the attack, and bayonet charges over open ground were emphasized. The cult of the offensive prevailed over concern for the defence, for which there was one standard: ground gained must be held at all costs.

Under the tutelage, direction and example of its German ally, the Ottoman Army adopted these tenets wholesale, and consistently undertook offensive actions throughout the 1915 Gallipoli campaign in repeated attempts to storm the Allied beachheads and drive the invaders back into the sea, as opposed to letting them exhaust themselves on prepared defences. At critical moments, Kemal's counter-attacks against the ANZAC landings on 25 April, and his unleashing of the massed assault that drove the Allies off the heights at Chunuk Bair on 10 August, were successes that vindicated the German emphasis on the need for individual officers to show initiative and boldness, even when the outcome of the battle was in doubt. Between these exemplars, however, the Ottoman Army's cult of the offensive succeeded in nothing more than a profligate waste of the lives of its officers and men. This was particularly the case during the Ottoman counter-offensive directed against Anzac Cove on 19 May. Ottoman troops, with fixed bayonets and shouting 'Allahu Akbar!' ('God is Great!') charged in close ranks during broad daylight against massed ANZAC rifles and machine guns only to be mowed down in wave after wave for almost no effect. The Ottomans incurred 13,000 casualties in the attack, including 3,000 killed; ANZAC casualties were 160 killed and 468 wounded. The massacre was so comprehensive that both sides had to agree to a temporary truce in order to clear the field of the Ottoman dead.

The Ottoman military did, though, seek to adapt to the evolving realities of combat. Reflecting the critical emphasis on firepower over manpower, in 1917, Ottoman infantry divisions in Palestine were restructured to incorporate a machine-gun company in every infantry battalion. That same year saw each infantry division divested of its best troops for the formation of a 50-man assault detachment (*hücüm müfrezesi*) to spearhead offensive operations at the tactical level. After completing a one-month assault training course, these elite units, modelled on the Imperial German Army's stormtroopers (*Stosstruppen*), received better rations and a distinctive badge (an embroidered hand grenade). Later, the divisional assault detachments matured into full assault battalions (*hücüm tabur*).

ANZAC

The standard weapon of the AIF was the .303 Short Magazine Lee-Enfield (SMLE) No. 1 Mk III bolt-action rifle, issued with the Pattern 1907 bayonet. These rifles and bayonets were originally of British manufacture; Australia's Small Arms Factory at Lithgow had commenced production of SMLEs in 1912, but its facilities were unable to produce the volumes of rifles and bayonets required in wartime until late 1915. Lithgow-manufactured rifles only began reaching Australian forces in quantity during 1916.

The British also supplied the AIF with its standard medium machine gun, the .303 Vickers Mk I, a liquid-cooled weapon capable of firing 450–500rd/min up to 2,000m. Reflecting awareness – from bitter experience – of the necessity for enhanced firepower, by 1916 each Australian light-horse regiment, which

Marksmanship training in New South Wales during World War I. Australia's transition to a professional as opposed to citizen-soldier military establishment was a slow one. The Defence Act of 1903 that came into effect on 1 March 1904 restricted military service to Australian soil, meaning any force contribution to an overseas commitment would be made from volunteers, and an expeditionary force for overseas service would have to await the outbreak of war to trigger its creation. At the outbreak of World War I, there were only 2,906 personnel in the professional force, compared to 50,332 in the militia. Little priority had been given to staff training and development, as it was assumed that British Army professional officers would be available if needed. This would hamper the Australian Army at all levels in 1914, when few Australians were qualified for senior staff appointments. (Paul Thompson/FPG/Archive Photos/Getty Images)

began World War I with two Maxim guns, had formed machine-gun sections, equipped with 12 Vickers guns, to accompany each regiment. The sections were later amalgamated under brigade control in much the same way as occurred with machine-gun companies being amalgamated to form battalions in the AIF. By 1917, every troop in each Australian light-horse regiment had been issued the .303 Lewis Mk I light machine gun and by the end of World War I each troop also had a strip-fed .303 Hotchkiss Mk I light machine gun, which increased the mobile firepower of each regiment. The NZMR Brigade evolved in a similar direction, being outfitted with one

Hotchkiss gun per troop, or four per squadron, by the end of the war. The Lewis gun was first used by specially created machine-gun sections of the New Zealand infantry at Ismailia, Egypt, in January 1916, ultimately becoming the standard infantry platoon-level support weapon providing automatic firepower during the tactical assault.

As befitting young and thinly populated dominions, ANZAC force structure was defined by adherence to the British imperial model. ANZAC tactical doctrine was heavily inculcated with the cult of the offensive, as derived from the British military establishment. Refusing to accept the reality that modern firepower – rifles, machine guns and quick-firing artillery – had rendered close-order assaults obsolete, the standard text insisted that closing with the enemy at all costs was paramount, achieved by moving in bounds and culminating in a bayonet charge. Victory was intended to be total; once an enemy line was broken, the advantage had to be followed up and the initial breakthrough consummated in annihilation. Maintaining the fastest possible pace of the assault was the key to victory, while utilizing existing terrain features for cover or going to ground to hold a forward position was actively discouraged. The contradictions between these directives and the actual nature of combat during World War I, particularly in a confined geographic environment such as the Gallipoli Peninsula, became readily apparent. Adapting to this reality, ANZAC troops learned to rely on concentrated firepower at close quarters, including the use of grenades, and adopted a 'bite and hold' approach to seizing and holding limited, attainable objectives. The structural advantages inherent to the defence, however, rendered any and all attempted alternative approaches, including the use of underground saps to approach Lone Pine and a night-time operation in a bid to seize the heights of Sari Bair, ultimately unsuccessful. Nevertheless, the experience was not wasted. In the Sinai and Palestine, these lessons would be applied in a much more favourable context, where the open environment would enable both the concentration of heavy firepower at a specific point and the utilization of mobility on the flanks to create the conditions for victory.

Australian grenade training in the Dardanelles, September 1915. Grenades – considered so irrelevant to the realities of modern battle that they were not even mentioned in the standard training manuals for the militaries on both sides prior to the outbreak of World War I – proved critical to the actual conduct of combat operations at Gallipoli, where fighting was at close quarters in cramped conditions. Landing without grenades, the ANZACs were forced to improvise, frantically manufacturing jerry-rigged explosives dubbed 'jam-tin bombs' for the front lines. These were always in short supply, however, and the ANZACs were constantly at risk of being bombed out of trenches, particularly during the savage fighting for control of Lone Pine. Ottoman troops, by contrast, were well-provided for; their assaults were preceded by a shower of grenades, which would continue throughout the action. (Daily Mirror Archive/Mirrorpix/Mirrorpix via Getty Images)

Lone Pine

6–10 August 1915

BACKGROUND TO BATTLE

The Allied landings commenced under cover of darkness early on the morning of 25 April. While the French made a diversionary landing at Kum Kale on the Asian shore, the British landed at Cape Helles at the tip of the peninsula. The ANZACs were tasked with landing further north, at Gaba Tepe on the Aegean coast, then advancing across the peninsula to the Dardanelles Straits, thereby cutting off the Ottoman garrison at Cape Helles.

In the event, the British failed to expand their toehold at Cape Helles. The ANZACs initially made progress, but as they began advancing without cover uphill into the never-ending expanse of ridges and gullies that defined the region, they became dispersed and increasingly vulnerable to counter-attacks from the Ottoman reinforcements now moving into their sector. After their repeated attempts to eradicate the ANZAC beachhead were bloodily repulsed, the Ottomans also adopted a defensive posture.

A series of costly British defeats at Cape Helles – the three battles of Kirithia on 28 April, 6–8 May and 4–6 June – proved there was no possibility of an Allied breakout from this sector. To circumvent the persisting stasis on the peninsula and restore strategic mobility, Hamilton resolved on a fresh landing at Suvla Bay, north of Anzac Cove. In support of this operation, the ANZACs would stage offensive actions of their own. The New Zealanders would spearhead an attempt to storm the Sari Bair Range commanding the Straits, while the Australians would concentrate on the lower ground of 400 Plateau, where Ottoman defences centred at Lone Pine. Colonel Nevill Maskelyne Smyth's 3,000-man strong 1st Australian Infantry Brigade, serving in Major-General Harold Bridgwood Walker's 1st Australian Division, was tasked with taking Lone Pine.

Troops land at Anzac Cove. While the 25 April landing operation appeared feasible on paper, in reality the inherent confusion of a pre-dawn amphibious landing, inadequate maps, rugged terrain, poor command choices and stiffening Ottoman resistance meant that none of the original objectives were achieved. General Sir Ian Hamilton, commander of the Mediterranean Expeditionary Force (MEF), refused to countenance evacuation, however, ordering his troops to dig in. (© Hulton-Deutsch Collection/CORBIS/Corbis via Getty Images)

In order to maximize their chances, the Australians incorporated three supporting features into their operational plan: an artillery barrage; the projection of underground tunnels forward from The Pimple (a bulge in the Australian line, hence the name) to create jumping-off points for the assaulting infantry as close as possible to the enemy trenches; and the laying of three mines.

The constricted space of The Pimple could not accommodate the whole of the 1st Australian Infantry Brigade, so only three of its four battalions

Anzac Cove today. Although partially sheltered from direct enemy observation, the site was in range of, and under constant threat from, an Ottoman artillery battery at Gaba Tepe, sardonically dubbed 'Beachy Bill' for its intermittent but dangerous shellfire. (Author's Collection)

would be committed to the initial attack. The assault would be launched in three successive waves, each composed of about 200 men from each of the three battalions. Each of the three lines thus consisted of roughly 600 men, equating to about seven Australians for every metre of Ottoman front-line trench to be stormed. The first wave would consist, from north to south, of the men of the 4th, 3rd and 2nd battalions attacking simultaneously along the whole front, with the second and third waves following about 50m behind them. The first wave would be launched from the secret underground saps, which were now less than 50m from the Ottoman front line. The second and third waves would launch their successive charges from The Pimple.

The assault by the three attacking lines of the 2nd Battalion would be led by 34-year-old Major Arthur Borlase Stevens. B Company, led by 21-year-old Captain John Henry Francis Pain, would jump off from the secret underground trench; C Company, under 25-year-old Major Leslie James Morshead, and D Company, under 25-year-old Captain Garnet Wollesley Brown, would launch their attack at the same time, but further back from the front-line trenches at The Pimple. The battalion reserve – A Company, under 29-year-old Captain George Sydney Cook (the son of former Prime Minister Joseph Cook, who had led Australia into the war) – would move up into the underground line as soon as B Company had commenced the attack.

Operational orders issued to the 1st Australian Infantry Brigade on 5 August instructed the men to leave their backpacks behind; the only things each man was to take with him were his rifle, bayonet, 200 rounds of ammunition, two days' food rations, one day's iron rations, a full water

bottle and two empty sandbags. All battalions' machine guns were to be forwarded to Lone Pine as part of the initial attack, along with 3,500 rounds of ammunition. Jam-tin-bomb sections were organized by company, each consisting of one rifleman in front, followed by one bomb-thrower and one bomb-carrier directed by an NCO, who would be supported by a second bomb-thrower, a second bomb-carrier, and a soldier with two haversacks full of bombs and 50 rounds of ammunition bringing up the rear. The total number of about 1,200 bombs allotted to the 1st Australian Infantry Brigade for this attack was recognized well prior to the assault as being insufficient; men were advised to scavenge grenades from the dead and wounded whenever possible.

On 4 August, two days before the offensive was to be launched, the artillery bombardment began, the task of cutting the Ottoman barbed wire being assigned to the New Zealand field artillery. Unprecedented in scale for Gallipoli, the bombardment was insignificant by Western Front standards. The total expenditure of shells amounted to just 211 (only nine of which were high-explosive) from the 18-pdr guns and 177 from the 4.7in, 5in and 6in howitzers. These did succeed in cutting the barbed wire in front of the Ottoman lines, but the lack of high-explosive shells meant the heavy overhead log-and-earth roofs of the trenches at Lone Pine remained mostly intact.

At 1400hrs on 6 August the three mines were detonated. The hour-long 'intensive' artillery bombardment that commenced at 1630hrs involved just eight guns focusing on Lone Pine itself, with around double that number shelling the flank and rear positions, delivering roughly one shell for every 115 square metres. The guns of the Royal Navy armoured cruiser HMS *Bacchante* joined in, targeting the Ottoman batteries and positions located further to the rear along Third Ridge.

Well-equipped Ottoman troops at Gallipoli. Responsibility for the Ottoman defence of 400 Plateau devolved upon Colonel Rüştü Bey, 16th Division, who had deployed two battalions of the 47th Regiment (approximately 1,000 men under Major Tevfik Bey) at Lone Pine itself, while its third battalion was stationed along Sniper's Ridge, a southern spur of the plateau. The headquarters of the 47th Regiment was located in a depression behind Lone Pine called The Cup. A battalion from the 57th Regiment was stationed further back in divisional reserve on Mortar Ridge. Just to the north, the 125th Regiment held Johnston's Jolly, while the 48th Regiment occupied its southern flank along Pine Ridge, a major inland extension of the plateau running south towards Gaba Tepe. (FPG/Hulton Archive/ Getty Images)

MAP KEY

1 1730hrs, 6 August: The Australian assault commences. The 4th Battalion takes and holds Aylward's Post, anchoring the left (northern) flank of the Australian advance. Other 4th Battalion detachments advance to McDonald's Post, Mackay's Post and Lloyd's Post.

2 1730hrs, 6 August: The 3rd Battalion seizes and holds Sasse's Sap and Woods's Post. Some men from the 3rd Battalion advance as far as Goldenstedt's Post, deep into the rear Ottoman lines leading directly to their headquarters in The Cup. The battalion also seizes and holds Tubb's Corner.

3 1730hrs, 6 August: The 2nd Battalion seizes and holds Pain's Post, anchoring the right (southern) flank of the Australian advance. Other 2nd Battalion detachments advance to Youden's Post, Cook's Post and Jacobs's Post.

4 1100hrs, 7 August: Ottoman counter-attacks force the Australians out of Mackay's Post and Lloyd's Post.

5 1400hrs, 7 August: Ottoman counter-attacks push the Australians out of Youden's Post and Cook's Post.

6 1000hrs, 8 August: Ottoman counter-attacks force the Australians to withdraw from Goldenstedt's Post.

7 1200hrs, 8 August: The Australians bolster their defences in the centre of the line by digging a trench connecting Sasse's Sap with Woods's Post.

8 1900–2300hrs, 8 August: In desperate fighting, the Australians repulse Ottoman attempts to storm Jacobs's Post.

9 0630hrs, 9 August: Ottoman troops take Sasse's Sap, only to be driven out again by an Australian counter-attack.

10 1100hrs, 9 August: Jacobs's Post changes hands multiple times before the Australians are finally forced to withdraw.

11 10 August: The Australians are exhausted but the Ottomans are overstretched fighting simultaneous actions at Chunuk Bair and Suvla Bay. Both sides hunker down to consolidate their existing front lines.

Battlefield environment

The Ottoman front line on 400 Plateau snaked around its eastern edge from Johnston's Jolly to Lone Pine. Owen's Gully separated the northern part of Lone Pine from Johnston's Jolly, although communication trenches running down into the gully connected the two. Each was defended by a number of front-line and secondary trenches as well as supporting and communication trenches. The centre of the Ottoman firing line was set back from both strong flanking strongholds, allowing enfilade fire to be brought to bear on the attackers as they swept past towards the centre of the line. This part of the position was not as heavily entrenched as the flanks and for a length of about 50m the front-line trench was open with no head cover. Strongly fortified, like its northern flanks, with sandbags, mud bricks, earthen embankments, thick log head covers and at least one machine-gun post, the southern sector was on a slightly higher elevation, leaving many of the Australian attackers exposed to ongoing Ottoman machine-gun fire and shrapnel as they searched for a way to penetrate the works.

The approach across no man's land, up to 100m wide and labelled the Daisy Patch, from the adjacent bulge in the Australian line – sardonically dubbed The Pimple – would not be easy. The 250m width of the Ottoman front line at Lone Pine was heavily defended with strong barbed-wire entanglements, the trenches in some parts covered with thick timbers and layers of earth. Added to this, Ottoman machine guns swept the approach, as did artillery batteries entrenched along Third Ridge, just over 1km to the rear.

One of the 3rd Battalion's objectives beyond the Ottoman front line was a trench later known as Sasse's Sap; it would help form the central defensive line held by the Australians at Lone Pine. This length of trench lay completely open to Ottoman enfilading fire from Johnston's Jolly, as there were no transverse bends built into it. A narrow communication trench, heading east towards the edge of the plateau, had been dug into the southern end of Sasse's Sap, and at right angles to it. From this trench three additional saps ran forward. The third sap, which now represented the deepest penetration of the new Australian front line, terminated close to the eastern edge of the plateau looking down directly into the Ottoman reserve areas in The Cup. This was occupied by Sergeant Major Paul Goldenstedt and his men, and would become known as Goldenstedt's Post.

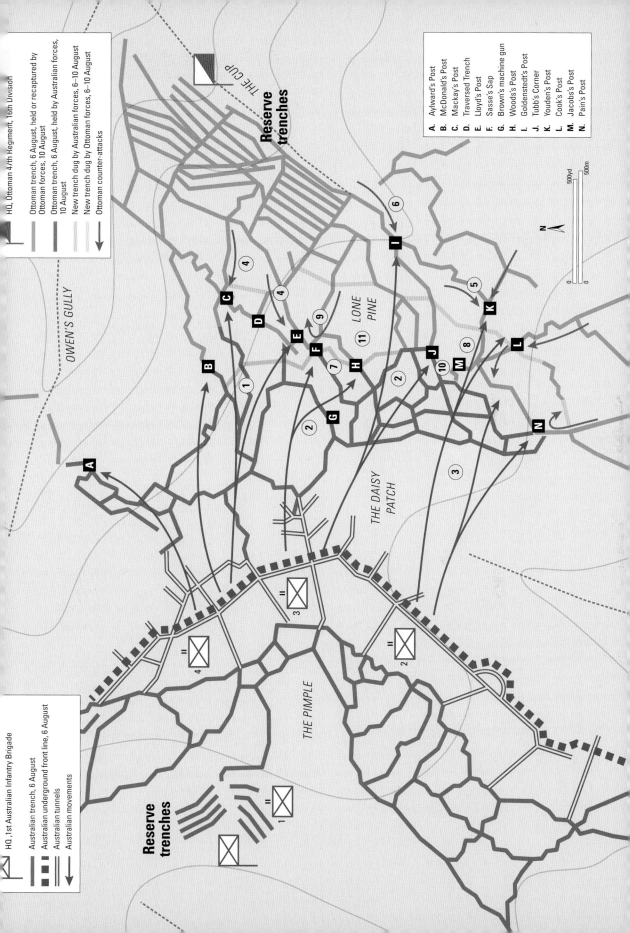

OWEN'S GULLY

THE CUP

Reserve trenches

Reserve trenches

THE PIMPLE

THE DAISY PATCH

LONE PINE

HQ, Ottoman 4th Regiment, 16th Division

Ottoman trench, 6 August, held or recaptured by Ottoman forces, 10 August

Ottoman trench, 6 August, held by Australian forces, 10 August

New trench dug by Australian forces, 6–10 August

New trench dug by Ottoman forces, 6–10 August

Ottoman counter-attacks

HQ, 1st Australian Infantry Brigade

Australian trench, 6 August

Australian underground front line, 6 August

Australian tunnels

Australian movements

A. Aylward's Post
B. McDonald's Post
C. Mackay's Post
D. Traversed Trench
E. Lloyd's Post
F. Sasse's Sap
G. Brown's machine gun
H. Woods's Post
I. Goldenstedt's Post
J. Tubb's Corner
K. Youden's Post
L. Cook's Post
M. Jacobs's Post
N. Pain's Post

N

500yd

500m

A B C D E F G H I J K L M N

INTO COMBAT

At precisely 1730hrs, the ANZAC artillery bombardment lifted and in the ensuing silence three whistle blasts announced the commencement of the attack. Within seconds, three waves of 600 men each scrambled from the Australian trenches into no man's land. The secret subterranean saps served their intended purpose, effectively halving the gap between The Pimple and Lone Pine; even so, the Ottoman defenders quickly recovered from their surprise.

The 4th Battalion's objective was to capture the northern part of Lone Pine. Lieutenant-Colonel Charles Melville Macnaghten and his men entered the Daisy Patch and immediately presented an excellent field of fire for the Ottomans, especially for the artillerymen on Third Ridge, who could clearly see the waves of Australians charging across terrain bare of even the thick low scrub that covered its flanks. To make matters worse, these men were under complete enfilade from Ottomans entrenched at Johnston's Jolly to their left, across Owen's Gully. Tasked with capturing the central part of Lone Pine, the 3rd Battalion also faced enfilade from the Ottomans entrenched at Johnston's Jolly. Stevens was in command of the three attacking waves of the 2nd Battalion, ordered to capture the southern part of Lone Pine. The Australians were open to oblique fire from the south, from the Ottomans along the upper parts of Pine Ridge and Sniper's Ridge.

Those Australians who survived the charge across no man's land to reach the Ottoman front line found it inaccessible in many places because of the logs providing cover to the Ottoman trenches, many of which had survived the artillery bombardment. Caught out in the open, many of the Australians opted to continue on to the rear trenches, while others were determined to claw their way into the Ottoman front line. Lieutenant Arthur McKellar Giles and his men of the 4th Battalion were the first to reach the northern flank of Lone Pine, which was heavily timbered over. Their objective was to secure this sector, to block Ottoman reinforcements arriving from Johnston's Jolly. An Ottoman machine-gun team was eliminated when Private George Hayward slipped three jam-tin bombs into the opening in the head cover where the machine gun was located, wrecking the weapon and killing the team. The enemy still held a covered sap running off to their left, however, which halted the Australian advance. Giles took command, ordering his bomb-throwers to lead the assault by hurling jam-tin bombs into the sap entrance. The position was stormed, and with the Australians now swarming into their forward trenches the Ottomans in this sector fell back into Owen's Gully. Giles was killed in this action, command transitioning first to Captain Stewart Milson and then, after he was killed, to Lieutenant Richard Thomas Francis Seldon, who had lost an eye in the charge across no man's land, before he too was killed. Joseph William Aylward, a 22-year-old lance corporal, now assumed authority in this sector.

About 50m to the south Major Iven Giffard Mackay and his men, who had also ignored the front trench and pushed on to the next line of trenches close to the northern edge of the plateau, succeeded in blocking the other sap running down into Owen's Gully, consolidating their hold over the north-

eastern sector of the new Australian position in Lone Pine – soon known as Mackay's Post.

Lieutenant William Thomas McDonald (who had been wounded by a bayonet thrust) and his men took up a position halfway between Aylward and MacKay. McDonald could offer enfilade fire in support of Aylward, while Mackay would be able to offer similar support to McDonald – if each had been aware of the other's position, which at this stage was doubtful. In any event, McDonald was soon fully preoccupied with repelling desperate Ottoman efforts to storm his ad hoc barricade.

Captain Edward Acton Lloyd arrived to support MacKay, whose sap led down into Owen's Gully and was an extension of the second-line trench he now occupied. For some reason it was dubbed Traversed Trench (it was a long and straight passageway and not traversed at all) and would be occupied by a small detachment under 20-year-old Lieutenant James Bloomfield Osborne. Lloyd and his men pushed for a short distance into the sap to his front, which shortly veered north-eastward and ran just east of Traversed Trench before it too fell into the sides of Owen's Gully. The Ottomans along Johnston's Jolly completely enfiladed this trench, so at the very edge of the plateau Lloyd

An Ottoman command team and emplaced artillery piece at Gallipoli. When the Australian assault went in, Lieutenant-General Esat Pasha, commander of the Ottoman Army's III Corps, sent the 15th Regiment forward, and ordered Lieutenant-Colonel Ali Riza Bey of the 13th Regiment to take command of Ottoman forces at Lone Pine, with instructions to retake the front-line trenches. At 1900hrs, three battalions – 1st Battalion, 57th Regiment; 2nd Battalion, 13th Regiment; and 3rd Battalion, 47th Regiment – were mustered for the counter-attack. (Underwood Archives/ Getty Images)

and his men set about building a barricade, which would become known as Lloyd's Post. Lloyd attempted to reinforce Major Colin Douglas Austin, of the 3rd Battalion, in the communication trench to his right, but these detachments were wiped out, and Austin himself was killed in the mêlée.

Men of the 3rd Battalion, who had punched into the centre of the Ottoman line and pushed down the adjoining communication trenches and saps, quickly found that they were descending into The Cup, in Owen's Gully. This was a depression, a deep inlet branching at right angles off Owen's Gully in a southerly direction, which helped to define the rear part of the plateau on which the Ottoman trench systems of Lone Pine had been dug. The men had been ordered not to descend into these gullies, toward the Ottoman headquarters in The Cup; those who tried were wiped out. Others near the eastern edge of the plateau began to build barricades, while reinforcements behind them followed the trenches and saps along the northern and eastern edge of the plateau. Some remained above the parapets in no man's land, firing into the Ottoman soldiers who were bolting down the avenues of trenches and saps, heading for the rear. These Australians then clambered into the trenches, turned around and made their way back towards the covered front lines.

A critical objective for the men of the 3rd Battalion was to capture a series of trenches just beyond the front line, one subsequently dubbed Sasse's Sap. With their men, 23-year-old Sydney clerk Captain Donald Ticehurst Moore and 31-year-old Maitland schoolteacher Lieutenant Stanley Millwood Garnham approached Sasse's Sap from the covered flanks and were firing into it as Ottoman soldiers tried to escape to the rear. Moore ordered his men into the uncovered trench, and within minutes of its capture a barricade had been built along its northern length. This barricade was short of Lloyd's Post, which lay about 15m further north, and was positioned where a sap from the east ran at right angles to it. This exposed part of Sasse's Sap, between the barricade and Lloyd's Post, remained unoccupied by either side. Any attempts by the Australians to occupy this length of trench only provoked devastating enfilade fire from the Ottomans entrenched on Johnston's Jolly.

Lieutenant David Richmond Brown arrived with his sole surviving machine-gun crew, positioning them above open ground immediately behind Sasse's Sap, with a perfect view across Owen's Gully, only about 200m away, to a communication trench on Johnston's Jolly packed with Ottoman soldiers. Australian firepower tore up the trench, leaving it blocked with dead and dying – as with much of Lone Pine, the Ottomans had failed to dig transverse bends here for protection from being enfiladed. An Ottoman shrapnel shell from Third Ridge finally brought an end to this venture, most of the machine-gun crew and the men around them being hit and the gun itself destroyed. The Australians managed to beat back the Ottoman counter-attack against Sasse's Sap, however, and hurriedly continued to barricade the communication saps and build firing steps into what had been the rear of the trench.

The very end of the eastern-running trench from Sasse's Sap did not run off into Owen's Gully but terminated close to the very edge of the plateau. It was here at this sap, which represented the backbone to the three forward covering saps, that men from the 3rd Battalion, under the command of 23-year-old Cootamundra painter Lieutenant Sidney Albert Pinkstone,

This military decoration for gallantry in battle awarded by the Ottoman Empire, officially titled the Ottoman War Medal and unofficially dubbed the Iron Crescent (an allusion to the Iron Cross awarded by the empire's German ally), was mistakenly referred to as the Gallipoli Star by ANZAC troops who only became familiar with it when it began to be taken as souvenirs from enemy dead and prisoners of war during the Sinai and Palestine campaigns. While it does feature the date 1333 in the Islamic calendar (equivalent to the year 1915 in the western Gregorian calendar) it was in fact instituted by Sultan Mehmed V on 1 March 1915, prior to the first landings at Gallipoli on 25 April. The medal features the cypher of Sultan Mehmed V and characters representing the words 'The Victorious'. (The State Library of New South Wales)

established a defensive position by expanding and deepening the trench end. Pinkstone's position, later called Tubb's Corner, now represented the extreme right flank of the 3rd Battalion, and like Goldenstedt's Post was well forward of the Australian main defensive line. Given the tactical significance of Pinkstone's position, a number of men were rushed in to help ensure its incorporation into the Australian lines.

The first to reach the position later to be known as Jacobs's Post was Sydney clergyman Lieutenant Everard Digges La Touché and his small party of men. Another detachment under 30-year-old farmer Lieutenant Herbert Alexander Youden advanced up the left-hand fork of a Y-intersection just north of this sap and fought their way forward, utilizing everything from sandbags to the enemy dead to construct a rudimentary barricade, Youden's Post, which would anchor the south-eastern corner of the Australian perimeter at Lone Pine. A little further south, having taken the right-hand fork, Captain Cook and his men pushed forward and were able to consolidate at Cook's Post, a short distance back from the edge of the plateau. The most southerly part of the Australian defensive perimeter at Lone Pine was held by the already wounded Captain Pain and his men. He would hold Pain's Post with his few survivors until he was again wounded and evacuated.

Throughout the preliminary artillery bombardment Major Tevfik Bey had rotated most of his men back from the Ottoman forward trenches so as to minimize losses. This proved a boon to the first waves of the 1st Australian Infantry Brigade, who stormed the Ottoman front line before the bulk of the enemy could advance through the tunnels to reoccupy it. As the Australians penetrated deeper into the trenches, however, resistance stiffened. Ottoman troops improvised defensive positions at intersections, becoming aware they could anticipate an approaching Australian by the protrusion of his fixed bayonet. In several places dead Australians lay four or five deep at these junctions.

Even though there was now some form of continuous line connecting the forward parties of the 4th Battalion to the north with those of the 3rd Battalion at the centre, the men of the 2nd Battalion to the south were partially isolated. While the communication saps to their rear linked the three columns of the advance, the closest that the forward parties of the 2nd and 3rd battalions came in contact was at the positions at Tubb's Corner and Youden's Post, near the head of The Cup. These positions were separated by about 30m of no man's land; they needed to be bridged to form a forward defensive line. Until then small parties of Australians, with or without leaders, formed themselves into defensive pockets, establishing low sandbag barricades as best they could. These forward positions were far from secure against any coordinated Ottoman counter-attack, however, and if they fell the very heart of Lone Pine would be lost. It was obvious the gap between the 2nd and 3rd battalions had to be bridged – any concentrated Ottoman attack, at the centre of the Australian line, could shatter their defences. When Captain Cecil Duncan Sasse arrived at this part of the line with another company of the 1st Battalion, he was ordered to help men from the 3rd Battalion dig a firing trench connecting the isolated posts at Tubb's Corner and Youden's Post.

The Ottoman troops were in an equally parlous state. They now clung to the rearmost trenches of the plateau, occupying for the most part communication saps that were never designed for defence. The situation in the centre was extremely precarious, as the Australians had pushed close to the very edge of the plateau. The Australians could now use trench periscopes to look down Owen's Gully or Legge Valley and see Ottoman reinforcements moving up in a continuous stream. If ANZAC artillery could have shelled the area just behind Lone Pine it would have resulted in a slaughter. Although the Ottomans lost two regimental commanders – Major Ibrahim Şükrü of the 15th Regiment, and Major Tevfik Bey of the 47th Regiment, both mortally wounded by bombs – it was the Australians who were typically on the receiving end. At 2300hrs the Ottoman counter-attack went in and, after fierce hand-to-hand fighting, began to force the Australians back.

Aylward's Post at the northern extension of the Australian line was on the brink of being overwhelmed when at the last possible moment reinforcements arrived with a machine gun, forcing the Ottomans to withdraw. About 50m to the south-east, the wounded Major Mackay, whose isolated post had become a death trap, requested to Lieutenant-Colonel Macnaghten – who had been wounded in the knee by shrapnel – that he be allowed to evacuate the position. Macnaghten agreed and Mackay began withdrawing the survivors, though only from the hub and not the communication saps leading into it. He ordered that the head of these saps be barricaded while he alone remained in the trench bay to repel any Ottoman advance as the work was progressed.

To the south of the 4th Battalion's position, the commanding officer of the 3rd Battalion, Lieutenant-Colonel Ernest Samuel Brown, was killed by shrapnel shortly before dawn. At daybreak on Saturday 7 August, the

Australians were subject to a rain of grenades to which they could only make a feeble response, as their supply of jam-tin bombs was limited to a few sandbags' full. Lloyd had to clear out his post, holding the position himself with just one other man for nearly two hours until a fresh supply of grenades arrived.

Lieutenant Osborne, who commanded Traversed Trench, was seriously wounded, and the Australians were also driven out of Lloyd's Post, leaving those manning Traversed Trench cut off, with no-one left protecting its southern entrance. Now that Mackay's Post had been abandoned, the men in Traversed Trench were isolated forward of the Australian front line in this sector of Lone Pine, with both of their flanks completely exposed.

A counter-attack led by Captain Allan Humphrey Scott temporarily stabilized the situation, Scott and one of his men hurling jam-tin bombs across no man's land, and when these ran out, using improvised grenades, including 18-pdr shell cases filled with high-explosive. This succeeded in reclaiming Lloyd's Post, but with daylight it was now apparent the entire length of Traversed Trench was fully exposed to enfilading fire from Ottoman machine guns at Johnston's Jolly. If Traversed Trench could not be held, neither could Lloyd's Post. Scott ordered both evacuated and a new barricade established to their rear.

While the northern sector settled down into a static exchange of bombs and sniper fire, Ottoman pressure intensified against the centre and southern flank of the Australian salient in Lone Pine. Woods's Post represented the centre of the Australian line, and the Ottoman soldiers located in The Cup, just 25m distant, launched a frontal assault against it. The attackers were swept away by fire from an Australian machine gun, supported by enfilading rifle fire from Goldenstedt's Post. The Ottomans did not try this again, but

One Australian soldier uses a trench periscope while the other stands guard, bayonet at the ready. Far above and beyond its day-to-day frustrations with the improvisation, the heat, the flies, the diet and the diseases, service at Gallipoli was extremely hazardous. The 1st Battalion went into battle at Lone Pine on 6 August 1915 with 21 officers and 799 other ranks, and of them seven officers and 333 men would become casualties by 10 August. It was even worse for the 2nd Battalion – it entered the fight with 22 officers and 560 others, and on coming out, no fewer than 21 officers and 409 other ranks had become casualties. Among those wounded and evacuated to Alexandria was Captain George Sydney Cook, who recovered under the care and supervision of his wife, Elsie, then serving in Egypt with the Australian Army Nursing Service. (The State Library of New South Wales)

Dawn counter-attack

For the men of the 1st Brigade, 1st Australian Division, taking the Ottoman trenches opposite their lines at Lone Pine on 6 August 1915 would prove the easy part. Holding them would be the real challenge. Over the next four days, wave after wave of Ottoman counter-attacks would crash against makeshift Australian defences, with every square metre of ground being bitterly contested in desperate fighting. Here, Australian troops muster at a critical intersection as an Ottoman counter-attack occurs at dawn on 7 August. The pine logs that previously roofed the trench were either blown apart by the artillery barrage that preceded the Australian assault, or were ripped away by the attacking troops, and now lie discarded and scattered about. The Australians have constructed a firing step from the bodies of the trench's original occupants on its eastern side so they can fire over the parapet at the approaching enemy, Ottoman infantry charging across open ground. The Australians have established a firing line. A lieutenant is blazing away with his Webley Mk VI revolver, while his men aim their SMLE No. 1 Mk III bolt-action rifles, Pattern 1907 bayonets fixed for imminent close-quarters fighting. Grenades – the signature weapon of the struggle for Lone Pine – are flying in both directions. Lacking anything more than a limited supply of jerry-rigged jam-tin bombs with which to retaliate, the Australians are forced to hurl the incoming Ottoman grenades back at their wielders before they detonate, with the concomitant risk to fingers and hands.

they did continue to try to force the Australians out of this position with an ongoing bombing fight.

To the south, a determined Ottoman attack spearheaded by bombs was launched against Cook's Post, which was also subject to enfilading fire from Johnston's Jolly. The Australians had no grenades with which to retaliate. Desperate appeals were made to company headquarters for bombs, but none were to be had. The men caught the enemy's grenades as they fell and hurled them back before bursting. Many were killed, however, hands and arms being blown off as grenades exploded in the act of being thrown back at the Ottomans. The post rapidly became packed with dead and wounded.

An Ottoman assault at 1200hrs against Cook's Post was launched from the parallel trenches to its right and rear. Lieutenant-Colonel Robert Scobie, commanding 2nd Battalion, knew there was no way that Youden's Post and Cook's Post could be held and now ordered the survivors to get out while they still could. Scobie, who remained in one of the saps while the men withdrew to make sure none of the wounded was left behind, was subsequently killed. Command in this sector passed to Stevens.

Another Ottoman assault went in against Jacobs's Post. Rifle fire broke up the charge, but the survivors were able to take shelter in a shallow sap in the middle of no man's land. From this position they began to bomb Jacobs's Post and the saps leading back from Youden's Post and Cook's Post. Captain Harold Jacobs, 1st Battalion, who was unaware Scobie had earlier ordered the evacuation of Youden's Post and Cook's Post, was shocked to see Ottoman bayonets protruding above the parapets of these two positions, and the enemy now pushing down the communication trench leading from Cook's Post in a bid to reach their original front line. By 1300hrs it looked as if the southern part of the line must surely fall, and if it did, Lone Pine would have to be evacuated as it would be indefensible, given the main arteries of supply back to The Pimple would be in Ottoman hands.

Desperate efforts succeeded in establishing a continuous firing trench along the entire southern flank, which now stretched from the old Ottoman

front line to Tubb's Corner. An Ottoman assault against Goldenstedt's Post was repulsed, but after Jacobs had to be evacuated from Jacobs's Post with a head wound the Australians were nearly bombed out of the position, only the erection of a screen jerry-rigged out of chicken wire enabling them to hold on. Another massed Ottoman assault was then torn apart by ANZAC artillery battery fire as it swarmed across no man's land.

By nightfall the Ottomans had failed to retake their front-line trenches, but had pushed the Australians back from the head of The Cup, denying them visual access into the Ottoman reserve areas. The Australians did still hold Goldenstedt's Post, from which they continued to throw jam-tin bombs down into the head of The Cup, which exploded murderously among the Ottoman reinforcements waiting to be fed into the battle.

At dawn on Sunday 8 August another Ottoman assault against Jacobs's Trench was repulsed, but constant pressure forced the evacuation of Goldenstedt's Post. It was approaching 1000hrs and Colonel Smyth sent a message to Lieutenant-Colonel Harold Edward 'Pompey' Elliott, ordering the reserve 7th Battalion to move forward and relieve the men in the southern sector. Smyth, while acknowledging the stress under which the 3rd and 4th battalions had been placed during the last few days, decided to leave them in the central and northern sectors respectively, supported by the reserve 12th Battalion. At about midday, the wounded Major David McFie McConaghy began to supervise the urgent sapping that was required to bridge the gap between Sasse's Sap and Woods's Post. Lieutenant Tallisker Donald McLeod was sent over to Sasse's Sap to supervise the work there, while

An Australian Vickers gun at Gallipoli. With the situation at Lone Pine becoming critical, Captain John Henry Francis Pain was ordered to bring a machine gun into action to support Jacobs's Post. Pain set the gun up out in the open; to further increase the sweep of fire, he placed the legs of its tripod on the shoulders of his men, privates William Nichol, James Alexander Montgomery and William James Goudemey. Repeatedly wounded, Pain managed to fire nearly 1,000 rounds at the most critical point in the fight, bringing the Ottoman attack to a standstill. Miraculously, he and his men all survived and managed to escape.
(The State Library of New South Wales)

Lieutenant Percy William Woods would do likewise from the post bearing his name. Both officers were in the act of establishing the line to be taken for the digging when McLeod was hit in the head by a sniper's bullet and killed instantly. Within a matter of hours, the posts were connected by a firing trench, complete with a firing step. This added significantly to the defence of the centre of the line at Lone Pine.

By early afternoon on 8 August, Elliott's 7th Battalion was taking charge of the southern sector. Elliott divided his front between two companies to enable greater communications within smaller groups. The northern sub-sector, including the newly relocated Goldenstedt's Post and Woods's Post, were placed under the command of Lieutenant William John Symons. Lieutenant Gilbert Joseph Cullen Dyett would command the southern sub-sector, at Jacobs's Post and Jacobs's Trench. It was Dyett's positions that had been the focus of Ottoman counter-attacks attempting to recapture their front-line trenches. Elliott reinforced the three key defensive positions here. The first was defined by the eastern head of Jacobs's Post, which was now finally screened by bombproof wire netting. About 15m back, the post was further strengthened where the original head cover remained at Pain's Post, while the third position was located at the next transverse of the covered works. All three of these positions gave a clear field of fire over the lower ridges and gullies leading off Lone Pine to the south. The men in this sector were also supported by two machine guns.

These preparations were immediately tested when a heavy assault crashed against this sector. Ottoman Army III Corps commander Lieutenant-General Esat Pasha channelled reinforcements to Lone Pine from Gaba Tepe in the form of the 4th Battalion of the 77th Regiment. Colonel Rüştü immediately committed them to the counter-offensive. An Ottoman artillery barrage was followed by the now-standard shower of grenades and then rifles and bayonets. The man standing next to Elliott was shot in the head, splattering Elliott with blood and brains. Attacks continued all along the line all day and into the night. When darkness fell the heaviest pressure was concentrated against the Australian southern flank, between Jacobs's Post and Goldenstedt's Post. In response, Lieutenant Frederick Harold Tubb and his reserve company of the 7th Battalion at Brown's Dip were moved up as reinforcements. Savage hand-to-hand fighting ensued, with the momentum shifting constantly. It was 0200hrs before the Australians were able to secure the position.

That evening, Esat committed more reinforcements to the 16th Division – the 4th Battalion, 10th Regiment (4th Division) and the 12th Regiment (8th Division). Rüştü attacked with these fresh troops at 0500hrs on Monday 9 August, the Ottoman assault being heralded with an artillery barrage before the troops moved out of their trenches. Machine-gun fire swept the Australian lines, which were then inundated with grenades as soon as the Ottoman troops were within throwing range. At the northern flank of their attack, the Ottoman forces managed to drive the Australians out of Sasse's Sap, only for the Australians to recapture it minutes later and establish a new barricade. The Ottomans then stormed this position, forcing their way into the heart of Lone Pine, dangerously close to the advanced 1st Australian Infantry Brigade headquarters. Only desperate defence, incorporating everyone from the commanding officers to the brigade staff and walking wounded, forced the Ottomans out of the Australian lines. In one notable incident, 19-year-

old Private John Patrick Hamilton climbed up above the parapet and coolly shot down the Ottomans as they again attempted to bomb the Australians out of Sasse's Sap. He remained in no man's land for approximately six hours, yelling instructions to point out Ottoman targets. He was later awarded the Victoria Cross.

The defenders at Goldenstedt's Post resorted to using improvised grenades made from slabs of guncotton tied to a small board shaped like a hairbrush. Having successfully repelled the Ottomans, Symons was ordered by Elliott to help defend Jacobs's Post, while Tubb was made responsible for defending what was now called Symons's Post, the barricaded entrance to the trench that led to Goldenstedt's Post. One by one, the ten men holding this strongpoint were shot down or bombed out until only a wounded Tubb and two of his corporals, William Dunstan and Alexander Stewart Burton, remained standing. Without warning, the Ottoman troops detonated a demolition charge of guncotton, throwing the three men off their feet as the barricade and surrounding parapets collapsed into the trench all around them. Recovering, Tubb emptied his revolver into the Ottoman soldiers charging to follow up this opportunity, while Dunstan and Burton worked frantically to establish a new barricade. Both of them were taken out by grenades – Burton was killed, Dunstan was temporarily blinded by shrapnel – but they had bought enough time for reinforcements to arrive and secure the position. Tubb, Burton and Dunstan were all subsequently awarded the Victoria Cross.

A worse disaster unfolded at Jacobs's Post. During the night, the shallow sap just north of and parallel to Jacobs's Trench had been expanded, the intent

The 'Rising Sun' hat badge, worn by members of the Australian military to this day, originated in 1902 as a marker of identity for contingents raised after Federation for service in South Africa during the Second Anglo-Boer War. As illustrated here, the third iteration of the badge, first issued in May 1904, incorporated a scroll inscribed with the words 'Australian Commonwealth Military Forces' and was worn throughout both World Wars. (The State Library of New South Wales)

being to provide covering fire to the front line at the Australian southern perimeter. At its slightly higher elevation, however, this new trench would be clearly visible to the Ottomans stationed to the north on Johnston's Jolly. At dawn, the Australians lining the trench were simply mown down from behind by Ottoman machine guns. Ironically, the Australians' corpses, left neatly lined up leaning against the parapet, with hats and bayonets clearly visible, created the impression the trench was still manned, and the Ottoman forces to the south did not probe this sector.

At Jacobs's Post, Lieutenant West was wounded, and had to be evacuated. Elliott moved Lieutenant Harold Henry Young with six men forward as reinforcements; they found the position held by just one survivor, Private Leslie John Shadbolt. The entire defence, now only seven strong, was almost immediately killed or wounded. A platoon from the 12th Battalion under Lieutenant Thomas John Woodhouse was ordered into Jacobs's Trench, but before getting there he was killed and his reinforcements were overwhelmed, the Ottomans capturing Jacobs's Post and pressing dangerously close to Pain's Post. Elliott ordered his adjutant, 20-year-old Lieutenant Hector Ernest Bastin, to retake Jacobs's Post, which he accomplished, having an arm shattered by a bullet in the process. After another Turkish assault drove the Australians out, Elliott handed his own revolver to Symons and ordered him to retake Jacobs's Post; again the Australians succeeded, only to again be forced out by the incessant hail of Ottoman grenades, hurled from three directions as the Ottoman troops closed in for the kill on this position. Symons established a new barricade halfway between Pain's Post and Jacobs's Post and grimly held on, repelling wave after wave of Ottoman bayonet charges along the line of the trench, while those Ottoman soldiers who attempted to outflank them by advancing across no man's land above ground were cut down by enfilading fire from the surrounding Australian lines. For his courage and resolute leadership in holding Jacobs's Trench, which by the end of the action was carpeted in some places 1–1.5m deep in the dead and dying of both sides, Symons was awarded the Victoria Cross.

At midday the Ottomans tried another attack against the centre of the Australian lines and managed to capture parts of Sasse's Sap. Captain Sasse personally went in to clear them out, taking a rifle with fixed bayonet and three men carrying filled sandbags, which they used to make a low barricade from which Sasse could take cover and fire into the Ottoman troops. He was joined by Captain Alfred John Shout of the 1st Battalion and half-a-dozen soldiers carrying sandbags and jam-tin bombs. Together, they charged down the trench. Both officers ran abreast, with Shout throwing bombs and Sasse shooting down any Ottomans who did not flee. This activity continued until a bomb went off prematurely in Shout's hand, destroying it and mortally wounding him. For his actions he was awarded a posthumous Victoria Cross.

The survivors of the 4th Battalion were finally relieved by the men of the 2nd Battalion, and six officers and 150 troopers of the 7th ALH Regiment, just after dark on 9 August, while the 5th Battalion began to relieve the bloodied men of the 12th and 7th battalions. The 5th Battalion's Captain Robert Murdoch Finlayson Hooper was killed in similar circumstances to Shout as he too attempted to bomb Ottomans out of stubbornly held positions. By now, dead Australians were stacked in heaps in places where

there was available room and in other parts where there was no room they were left on the floor of the trench and covered with a thin layer of earth, which made a soft spongy floor to walk on. Ottoman corpses were piled up to help make bullet-proof parapets and also to make barriers to block communication trenches leading from the Ottoman reserve trenches.

Given the negligible amount of ground gained or conceded, the toll of dead, wounded or otherwise lost was horrific. The 1st Australian Infantry Brigade's battle for Lone Pine resulted in 2,277 Australian casualties, over 800 of whom were killed outright. Officers and men suffered indiscriminately; the 2nd Battalion lost over 70 per cent of its officers in the first 24 hours. Two battalion commanders were among the dead, while another received a serious wound early in the fight and an acting battalion commander suffered a nervous breakdown shortly after the battle. Unlike in most battles of World War I, few of the casualties at Lone Pine were from artillery fire; most physical wounds were the result of hand-to-hand fighting, including grenades, bayonets and small-arms fire. The percentage breakdown of Australians killed or wounded in the battle per battalion has been calculated as: 1st Battalion, 42 per cent; 2nd Battalion, 74 per cent; 3rd Battalion, 67 per cent; 4th Battalion, 64 per cent; 5th Battalion, 19 per cent; 7th Battalion, 51 per cent; and 12th Battalion, 16 per cent. Ottoman casualty figures made for similarly grim reading: 7,164 men were either killed, wounded, missing or taken prisoner.

Ottoman prisoners of war at Seddul Bahr. The Australians were stretched to the limit at Lone Pine, but the Ottomans had been pushed beyond the brink. With the struggle for Sari Bair raging and the landings at Suvla Bay yet to be contained, the defenders concentrated on neutralizing the more serious strategic threats elsewhere. Major Zeki Bey and his men, who had been fighting at Lone Pine for the last four days without rest, were finally withdrawn as both sides settled down to consolidate their new front line. Sappers on both sides continued a war of mine and counter-mine for months afterwards, but the stalemate persisted. (Interim Archives/ Getty Images)

Chunuk Bair

7–10 August 1915

BACKGROUND TO BATTLE

However bloody, the assault against Lone Pine was the only one of a series of diversionary probes intended to draw Ottoman attention away from the main thrusts of the Allied offensive that produced any concrete results. Attempts to seize ground at The Nek, German Officers' Trench, Dead Man's Ridge and Turkish Quinn's were total failures. The three mines dug under the Ottoman front lines at German Officers' Trench had been embedded too deep; their detonations only succeeded in alerting the enemy their positions were in imminent danger of attack. Ottoman retention of this position would have dire consequences, for the capture of German Officers' Trench before dawn was essential to avoid the threat of devastating enfilade fire into the ALH when they attempted to storm The Nek.

This action proceeded anyway, the narrow approach to The Nek, approximately the size of three tennis courts, compressing the charge of the ALH into four waves, each of 150 men, two waves from each regiment. The Ottoman positions were manned by elements of the 18th and 27th regiments, with the 57th Regiment plus the 72nd and 77th Arab regiments in reserve on Baby 700. A preliminary artillery barrage was intended to blast these units out of their trenches, but a seven-minute gap between the cessation of the barrage and the designated zero-hour for the assault meant the Ottoman trenches were fully occupied and waiting for the Australians when the first wave of the ALH went over the top, bayonets fixed, magazines empty, charging against concentrated machine-gun fire. Most did not make it 20m before being mown down. The subsequent three waves suffered an identical fate. It took less than 60 minutes for the ALH to incur more than 50 per cent casualties without gaining one square metre of ground. The ALH assault at adjacent

Dead Man's Ridge did at least succeed in breaking into the enemy front-line trenches but, unsupported, the Australians were swiftly bombed out by an Ottoman counter-attack. The mine embedded under Turkish Quinn's failed to detonate at all. Having been ordered to proceed with the scheduled attack anyway, the ALH were predictably slaughtered moments after they charged into no man's land.

Making these pointless sacrifices all the more tragic was the fact that they occurred in support of an operational plan that was already falling apart. General Sir Ian Hamilton's primary focus was to seize the heights of Sari Bair. This would be undertaken by two assault columns under the overall command of Major-General Sir Alexander John Godley. While Major-General Herbert Vaughan Cox's Left Assaulting Column, composed of Brigadier-General John Monash's 4th Australian Brigade and Cox's own 29th Indian Brigade, would seize Hill 971 (Koja Chemen Tepe) and Hill Q (Besim Tepe), the Right Assaulting Column, composed of the New Zealand Infantry Brigade (Canterbury, Otago, Wellington and Auckland battalions), supported by the majority of the 26th (Jacob's) Indian Mountain Battery and No. 1 Field Company of the New Zealand Artillery under Brigadier-General Francis Earl Johnston, would advance via Sazli Dere and Chailak Dere onto the Rhododendron Ridge and then to the vital high ground of Chunuk Bair, the dominant feature of the Sari Bair ridge line some 262m high. These objectives had to be taken in the six hours of darkness before dawn on 7 August.

In the event, these estimates would prove hopelessly optimistic. Precisely because the rugged terrain was considered essentially impassable, Ottoman Army high command did not anticipate an offensive in the Northern Group sector, which was defended by just two battalions, roughly 20,000 men drawn from the 19th, 5th and 16th divisions, clustered around strongpoints on Battleship Hill, Scrubby Knoll and Pine Ridge. Godley had approximately 37,000 men under his command, but these were tasked with advancing uphill at night into the sprawling heights of the Sari Bair ridge line, which consisted of sharp, rocky ridges, sheer cliffs, and a maze of narrow gullies (*deres*) cut by years of torrential rain. In many instances, forward progress was hand over hand, the Wellington Mounted Rifles Regiment (MRR) using their bayonets to cut steps in the steep clay slopes.

New Zealand soldier Private William James Batt poses with a unit mascot at Walker's Ridge, 30 April 1915. His state of undress and underfed condition were typical of ANZAC personnel at Gallipoli, where a poor diet and lack of access to fresh water directly contributed to the constant presence of endemic diseases throughout the campaign, particularly dysentery, which rendered units understrength and debilitated during the critical offensive actions at Lone Pine and Chunuk Bair; from 1 July to 5 August, an average of 73 men per day were reporting sick in the 1st Australian Division alone. (Hulton Archive/Getty Images)

1 Dawn, 7 August: After fighting their way uphill overnight, the New Zealand battalions assemble at The Apex, where Rhododendron Ridge and Cheshire Ridge meet.

2 1030hrs, 7 August: The Auckland Battalion launches an assault on the Ottoman positions at The Pinnacle. At great cost the Ottomans are pushed out, but the New Zealanders are unable to press on any further.

3 Early morning, 8 August: A pre-dawn bombardment shatters the Ottoman forces holding Chunuk Bair. When the Wellington Battalion goes over the top at 0415hrs it encounters almost no resistance as it seizes the summit.

4 0500hrs, 8 August: Lieutenant-Colonel William Malone, commanding the Wellington Battalion, consolidates the position, pushing two platoons forward as a screening force onto the forward southern slopes and landward eastern slopes, where they occupy empty gun-pits, and ordering a support trench dug on the reverse slope, above The Pinnacle.

5 0600hrs, 8 August: Before the New Zealanders can effectively entrench, intensifying Ottoman counter-attacks push the forward units out of the gun-pits. Malone orders a general withdrawal from the summit to the support trench on the reverse slope.

6 1600hrs, 8 August: Effectively isolated, Malone is killed by shellfire, attempts to reinforce the Wellington Battalion throughout the day having been compromised by Ottoman enfilading crossfire from the surrounding heights.

7 Night, 8/9 August: Under cover of darkness the Wellington Battalion is relieved and replaced by the Wellington MRR and the Otago Battalion.

8 Night, 9/10 August: Having sustained heavy casualties, the Wellington MRR and the Otago Battalion are pulled out of the line and replaced by two British 'New Army' battalions, 6th Loyal North Lancashire and 5th Wiltshire.

9 0430hrs, 10 August: Having been amassed in the sector, Ottoman reinforcements are unleashed in overwhelming numbers against the British troops holding Chunuk Bair, who are annihilated.

10 0600hrs, 10 August: Pouring over the crest and down the slope of Rhododendron Ridge, the Ottoman assault recaptures The Pinnacle. New Zealand troops manning The Apex are able to hold on to the position only after fierce hand-to-hand fighting finally halts the Ottoman charge.

Battlefield environment

The only practical route by which to approach Chunuk Bair ran almost directly east along a narrow saddle rising between Aghyl Dere to the north – where, a short distance from The Apex, there was a small sheltered plateau known as The Farm – and Sazli Dere to the south. Proceeding along this route would require displacing the Ottoman defenders at another knoll a further 100m from The Apex called The Pinnacle. From here it was a straight climb to the summit. Men advancing in daylight would be exposed to fire from Battleship Hill on the other side of Sazli Dere to the south, from the north, where Ottoman batteries were located behind the hills near the village of Anafarta Buyuk, and from Hill Q.

Echoes of the past: the contours of the trench lines that criss-crossed the ANZAC and Ottoman perimeters can still be observed on the peninsula today, at some points shockingly close together. Scattered throughout this terrain, the detritus of war is still being recovered – everything from spent rifle cartridges to fragments of human bone. (Author's Collection)

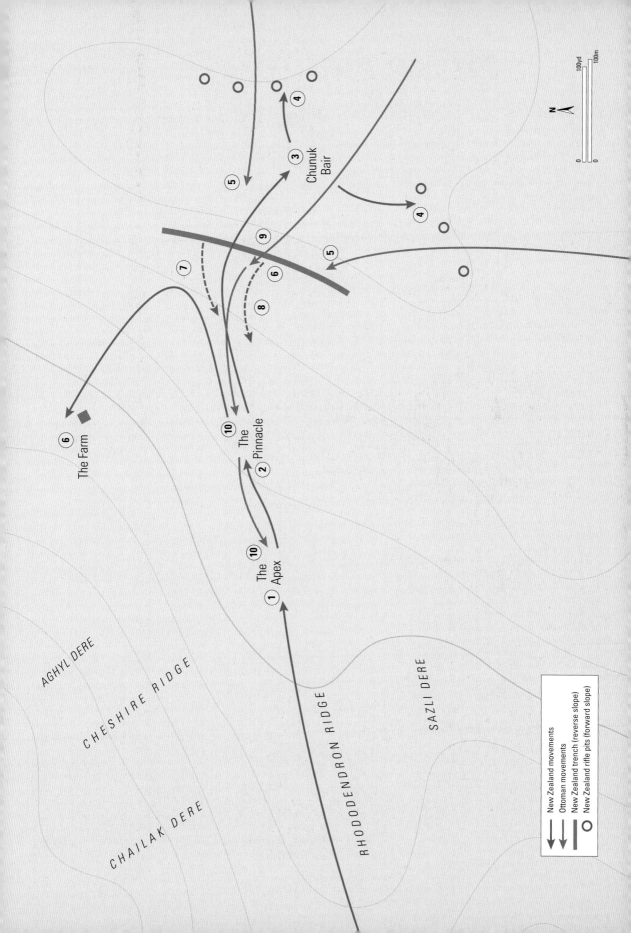

100yd
100m

N

Chunuk
Bair

④

⑤

③

④

⑤

⑨

⑦

⑥

⑧

The Farm

⑥

The
Pinnacle

⑩

②

The
Apex

⑩

①

AGHYL DERE

CHESHIRE RIDGE

RHODODENDRON RIDGE

SAZLI DERE

CHAILAK DERE

New Zealand movements
Ottoman movements
New Zealand trench (reverse slope)
New Zealand rifle pits (forward slope)

INTO COMBAT

The Right Assaulting Column made solid albeit slow initial headway through the foothills. The Auckland MRR swiftly captured an Ottoman stronghold dubbed the Old No. 3 Outpost in the centre. On their right, the Wellington MRR, with two platoons of the Māori Contingent attached, took Destroyer Hill and The Table Top. On the left flank, the Otago MRR and the Canterbury MRR advanced via Taylor's Hollow, Walden Point and Wilson's Knob to Bauchop's Hill, the feature furthest inland. The Otago MRR sustained the heaviest casualties during this phase of the operation, losing their commanding officer, Lieutenant-Colonel Arthur Bauchop, who was mortally wounded during the final bayonet charge; Lieutenant-Colonel John Findlay of the Canterbury MRR was also wounded, but survived.

Most of the Right Assaulting Column – the Otago, Wellington and Auckland battalions – now pushed eastwards up Chailak Dere to seize Rhododendron Ridge, where they were expected to link up with the Canterbury Battalion, proceeding up the valley to the south (Sazli Dere), in order to take Chunuk Bair. By this point the operation was already two hours behind schedule, however, and by the time the New Zealanders advanced onto Rhododendron Ridge as far as its confluence with Cheshire Ridge at a position dubbed The Apex, the sun had risen on 7 August.

Ottoman resistance was now stiffening. Unknown to ANZAC intelligence, the Ottomans had strong reserves on the north-western slopes of Hill 971 in the form of the 14th Regiment, under Lieutenant-Colonel Ali Rıfat, who had deployed his 1st Battalion in the outpost line along Table Top and Bauchop's Hill and his remaining two battalions on Abdul Rahman Ridge. As his 1st Battalion delayed the assault columns in the early hours of 7 August, Rıfat deployed his 3rd Battalion and two companies of the 2nd Battalion to the forward slopes of Abdul Rahman Ridge, blocking the 4th Australian Brigade, while the remaining 2nd Battalion companies were moved south to block the 29th Indian Brigade. Simultaneously, Major Mehmet Münir, commanding the 72nd Regiment, extended his lines northward to block the New Zealand Infantry Brigade. Esat also committed the 9th Division, under German Oberstleutnant Hans Kannengiesser, to this sector. Kannengiesser arrived at the Northern Group's Kemalyeri headquarters at 0440hrs, where he assumed command and stationed his 64th and 25th regiments on Hill Q.

Meanwhile, hesitation gripped the ANZAC officers at The Apex. Lieutenant-Colonel William George Malone, commanding the Wellington Battalion, opted to halt the advance and dig in. He wanted to hold off on any attempt to storm Chunuk Bair until the position gained by the Left Assaulting Column on the brigade's northern flank could be ascertained. Johnston arrived at the head of Chailak Dere sometime between 0600hrs and 0700hrs. He ordered the Auckland Battalion to advance against Chunuk Bair, but after assessing the situation the battalion's commanding officer, Lieutenant-Colonel Robert Young, recommended waiting until nightfall before attempting a further move forward. Johnston, Malone and Young discussed the matter, with Johnston finally agreeing that a daylight attack against the now-reinforced Chunuk Bair could not succeed.

Johnston reported to Godley at divisional HQ shortly after 0830hrs that it was not advisable to attack Chunuk Bair. Godley's response, received an hour later, was a terse, three-word directive: Attack at once. This laconic instruction was later supplemented by an order stating that the attack was to take place at 1030hrs, with artillery organized to support it. Major Arthur Cecil Temperley of the Otago Battalion begged Johnston to disobey the order, pointing out to him that this was an occasion when it was manifestly his duty to do so as he was the only real judge of the situation and assuring him that were Godley on the spot he would come to precisely the same conclusion. Johnston, however, refused to contemplate disobeying a direct order from a superior officer, and in any event, had he done so, Godley would probably have responded by relieving him of command.

At least the attack would not be made by the Auckland Battalion alone. After pushing up Aghyl Dere, several units from the 29th Indian Brigade of the Left Assaulting Force had finally linked up with the New Zealanders on Rhododendron Ridge. This included a company of 1st Battalion, 5th Gurkha Rifles, and two companies of 2nd Battalion, 10th Gurkha Rifles. Johnston stationed them on the Auckland Battalion's left, with the Canterbury Battalion in reserve.

The Auckland Battalion was drawn up in platoons in 12 lines, each 1m apart. The attack went in subsequent to an artillery barrage but before the brigade's machine guns under Captain Jesse Alfred Wallingford could be deployed in support. Charging uphill in broad daylight, the Auckland Battalion was rapidly shot to pieces by Ottoman crossfire, including the quick-firing mountain guns of the 8th Battery, 5th Artillery Regiment. The battalion's second-in-command, Major Samuel Alexander Grant, who led the charge from the front, was among the killed. The Auckland Battalion did succeed in driving the Ottomans out of The Pinnacle and occupying their trenches, but could make no further progress, being halted 275m from the summit of Chunuk Bair.

The situation in reserve was almost as disastrous. The commanding officer of the Canterbury Battalion, Lieutenant-Colonel John Gethin Hughes, was a Second Anglo-Boer War veteran and the first New Zealand recipient of the Distinguished Service Order, but his leadership in this operation had proved wanting. During the night approach he had become lost, with about half the Canterbury Battalion and its machine guns circling back to their starting point on Ocean Beach. Now, Hughes marshalled the battalion on the open crest of the ridge, in full view of the Ottomans higher up on Battleship Hill. They were subjected to a withering fire as they tried to advance towards The Apex; only 37 men made it that far.

When Johnston reported that the attack had failed, Godley did not insist on any further attempt to storm the heights. Hamilton was resigned to the fact that nothing more could be done until nightfall, and orders were issued at 1300hrs for consolidation of the positions taken by the two columns.

Kannengiesser meanwhile sent in his 25th Regiment to reinforce the battered 14th Regiment, but then suffered a serious chest wound and had to be evacuated. Fortunately for the Ottomans, the commander of the 4th Division, Lieutenant-Colonel Cemil, arrived at 9th Division headquarters after an all-night march to find that Esat had assigned him command of what

Born in Lewisham, England, on 24 January 1859, William George Malone emigrated to New Zealand in 1880, where he was active in farming, the law, politics and the military, serving in the New Zealand Armed Constabulary and the militia Volunteer Force and helping raise the Stratford Rifle Volunteers during the Second Anglo-Boer War. When the militia was succeeded by the Territorial Force in 1911, Malone, now a lieutenant-colonel, was appointed commander of the 11th Regiment (Taranaki Rifles). It was Malone who designed the 'lemon squeezer'-style hat that would later become standard issue for New Zealand service members. Upon the outbreak of World War I, he was appointed commander of the Wellington Battalion of the NZEF. Landing with his men at Gallipoli during the initial amphibious assault on 25 April 1915, he led them into action throughout the campaign. Fighting in the front-line trenches in the desperate struggle to hold Chunuk Bair, Malone was killed, possibly by friendly fire, on 8 August. (Historic Collection/Alamy Stock Photo)

was styled the Aghyl Dere Detachment (*Ağıl Dere Müfrezesi*), which was to be composed of Rifat's 14th Regiment, Kannengiesser's 25th and 64th regiments and Cemil's own 10th and 11th regiments. In the early hours of 8 August Cemil moved the 3rd and 4th battalions of his 11th Regiment into reserve positions behind the 25th Regiment and the battered 14th Regiment, and the 1st and 2nd battalions into the line to close the gap between the Aghyl Dere Detachment and Kemal's 19th Division.

Cemil intended to launch a counter-attack in order to push the New Zealanders off Rhododendron Ridge, but Lieutenant-Colonel Servet, the 64th Regiment's commanding officer, argued against the attack as any charge on the open slopes of this ridge would have to take place under the fire of the British land- and sea-based artillery. Even if the attack was successful it would be very costly and, if it failed, it would leave the gates to Chunuk Bair open for the New Zealanders to take advantage.

This conceded the initiative to Godley, who was already planning a renewed general assault at dawn along the whole line. This would be launched on the heights at 0415hrs, preceded by a 45-minute artillery bombardment. He ordered Johnston to renew the attack on Chunuk Bair, reinforcing the New Zealand Infantry Brigade with the British 7th (Service) Battalion, The Gloucestershire Regiment and the pioneers of 8th (Service) Battalion, The Welsh Regiment. On Johnston's left flank, Cox would take Hill Q with the 29th Indian Brigade and Hill 971 with the 4th Australian Brigade.

Again, the operation began to break down even before it went into effect. By dawn, Cox was still not yet in a position to attack; and when the forward units of the 4th Australian Brigade did advance they rapidly lost contact with each other. The already fractured offensive broke down completely as it encountered increasingly heavy Ottoman resistance. Monash reported to Cox that he had no option but to withdraw; by 0830hrs the brigade had pulled back to its start lines, having suffered in excess of 1,000 casualties for no gain. Cox's other units made little progress, grinding to a halt short of Hill Q at The Farm.

By contrast, the assault on Chunuk Bair proved a deceptively easy triumph. Johnston's assault was centred on the Wellington Battalion, with 7th Gloucestershire on the left and 8th Welsh on the right. The Auckland MRR, the Māori Contingent and the remnants of the Canterbury Battalion were ordered to support the attack if required, and moved to The Apex in readiness. The Otago Battalion would hold The Apex.

In the event, the preliminary artillery barrage proved decisive. The Ottoman 1st Battalion, 14th Regiment, which had been in constant combat since the initial attack on the evening of 6 August, simply disintegrated, and Johnston's subsequent infantry assault encountered almost no resistance as it scaled the heights of Chunuk Bair. Upon reaching the summit, Malone pushed two platoons forward as a screening force onto the forward southern slopes and towards the landward eastern slopes, where empty gun-pits were found and occupied by the New Zealanders. On the reverse slope, above The Pinnacle, Malone ordered a support trench dug. As the sun rose, the New Zealanders could see the white cottages of the village of Maidos, the Dardanelles Straits and the Asian shore beyond. It was, in both geographic and strategic terms, the highpoint of the campaign.

Kemal, who was headquartered with his 19th Division on Battleship Hill, could clearly see the crisis unfolding. He ordered two battalions of the 10th Regiment to drive Malone off the heights, but the exposed slopes of Battleship Hill were a prize target for ANZAC artillery, which brought the initial counter-attack to a standstill. Cemil now ordered Servet to take command of the entire line and restore the situation. The battle for control of Chunuk Bair now truly began, and would continue to rage throughout the day, as Ottoman units on the adjacent higher ground of Hill 971 and Hill Q kept up a sustained heavy fire against the isolated New Zealanders.

For the best part of an hour the Wellington Battalion had been largely unmolested as its men frantically sought to dig in, but owing to the hard and stony nature of the soil, and the fact that the majority of the New Zealanders had only entrenching tools, progress was very slow, and the trenches were not more than 65cm deep when the Ottoman counter-attack started. Preceded by showers of grenades, the enemy worked their way up the slope until they were able to fire into the gun-pits where the New Zealand advanced covering parties had been placed. These soon became untenable; only a few survivors made it back from the forward slopes.

The flat ground on the ridge at Chunuk Bair was extremely narrow, being only 13m across at its widest point, and the surrounding steep hills allowed the Ottomans to approach safely under cover, mustering right under the New Zealand positions before being detected. Some Ottoman soldiers would crawl to within 2m of the Wellington Battalion's forward trench before the defenders could spot the bayonets on their rifles and take blind shots at them, extending their rifles over the parapet and firing without putting their heads up to line the sights.

Having been pushed out of the Turkish trench on the crest, Malone pulled his men back to the support line 15m further down on the reverse slope. Here, the Wellington Battalion was able to fight off repeated Ottoman bayonet charges, gunning the enemy down as they poured in waves over the crest.

At 0900hrs, two companies from the Māori Contingent were sent forward but, after passing The Apex, they came under heavy fire from the direction of Battleship Hill, forcing them to take cover down in Aghyl Dere. They would not make it to Chunuk Bair, and were unable to support Malone, although they did succeed in linking up with Cox near The Farm. The two squadrons of the Auckland MRR also tried to get up to Chunuk Bair, but only made it as far as The Pinnacle. Wallingford dispatched four machine guns with their crews to the heights in support, and although three eventually made it, the guns were so badly damaged that they had to be cannibalized to make one working weapon. This gun, along with a captured Ottoman weapon, were the only machine guns Malone had on the summit; because of their exposed positions above the parapet, they would soon be put out of action.

Malone was effectively cut off from reinforcement, resupply and even communication. All of his dispatch-runners were soon killed or wounded; Herculean efforts by signal parties to lay telephone lines were constantly frustrated by Ottoman shellfire, which repeatedly cut the wires. Malone fought desperately to hold his tenuous position, ordering his men over the top in repeated bayonet charges to drive the enemy back. Armed only with an entrenching tool, time after time he conspicuously led from the front

The standard SMLE rifle used by ANZAC troops throughout World War I was issued with the British Pattern 1908 bayonet pictured here. British military doctrine at the outbreak of the war continued to insist firepower was only a preliminary to the decisive use of the bayonet at close quarters. While the bayonet did see action in close-quarters fighting, for example by the Australians at Lone Pine, the reality of 20th-century combat was defined by the weight of firepower that could be focused on a specific point; even at Lone Pine, the signature weapon was the bomb, not the bayonet. (History and Art Collection/Alamy Stock Photo)

whenever the Ottomans threatened to break through, wherever the action was hottest. He was killed by shellfire just after 1600hrs; so intense was the battery and counter-battery fire it is unknown whether this was Ottoman, ANZAC or Royal Navy. Major William Henry Cunningham assumed command.

It had been an exceptionally hot summer day, and the New Zealand soldiers had used up their meagre supplies of both grenades and water long before night fell. Under cover of darkness, the Wellington MRR and the Otago Battalion were ordered up and the shattered remnants of the Wellington Battalion – just 70 unwounded left out of the 760 who had originally occupied the crest – were finally relieved, filtering down and away from Chunuk Bair.

While ANZAC casualties mounted, Ottoman numbers continued to increase. With the landings at Suvla Bay contained and no further amphibious landings eventuating, at 0630hrs on 7 August Liman had ordered both the 7th and 12th divisions under the command of Colonel Ahmet Fevzi forward from their reserve positions at Bulair at the base of the peninsula. After a punishing forced march of 30km and 40km respectively, as soon as the forward elements of the two divisions arrived at the front lines they were ordered into the attack, without artillery support or even time to rest. When Fevzi objected, Liman removed him from command and replaced him with Kemal, effective at 2345hrs on 8 August. Lieutenant-Colonel Şefik of the 27th Regiment succeeded Kemal in command of the 19th Division.

Kemal's counter-attack duly commenced early on the morning of 9 August. In a series of meeting engagements commencing at 0400hrs, the 12th Division successfully repulsed several British attempts to seize the high ground at Tekke Tepe and Kiretch Tepe. Tasked with seizing the enemy positions on Damakjelik Bair (Damakçılık Bayrı), the 20th and 21st regiments of the 7th Division were less fortunate. The defences were strongly held by the 4th Australian Infantry Brigade, and the terrain channelled the attackers downhill into the ravine of Kayaçık Dere before they could make their assault uphill. The struggle raged from 0430hrs until a counter-attack at 1000hrs pushed the two regiments back down into Kayaçık Dere. The two regiments lost 978 officers and men, including both commanding officers, Lieutenant-Colonel Halit of the 20th and Lieutenant-Colonel Ziya of the 21st, who both died of their wounds two days later.

Hamilton was aware that the offensive had not met its strategic objectives, but was convinced even a limited breakthrough along the heights of Sari Bair constituted the key to victory; his hopes were now pinned on the roughly 600 New Zealanders grimly holding their tenuous grip on the reverse slope, withstanding wave after wave of Ottoman assaults. Lieutenant-Colonel Athelstan Moore of the Otago Battalion was soon wounded and passed command to Lieutenant-Colonel William Meldrum of the Wellington MRR. Already in desperate straits – fighting hand to hand to their front and enfiladed from both sides – the New Zealanders were not helped when, at 1700hrs, three misdirected British howitzer shells exploded in their ranks. Despite being himself wounded in the shoulder and neck, Meldrum rallied his men and led them in numerous counter-attacks that kept the Ottomans at bay.

The final British attempt to seize the heights of Sari Bair began at 1715hrs after a heavy bombardment. The attack went wrong from the start when several assaulting columns were delayed by the difficult terrain and only Major Cecil John Lyons Allanson's 1/6th Gurkha Rifles (29th Indian Infantry Brigade) made it to the summit, punching through the lines of the newly arrived Ottoman 24th Regiment, which had taken over the 64th Regiment's lines on the night of 8/9 August, to occupy Hill Q. Again, final victory seemed tantalizingly close; though wounded in the action, from this elevation, Allanson could see the Dardanelles Straits, and the Ottoman transport columns on the roads leading to Achi Baba. This illusion was not long sustained. Not only did reinforcements fail to reach Allanson, his Gurkhas were pounded by a salvo of heavy shells from misdirected Royal Navy guns offshore. Colonel Ali Reza was able to take advantage of the situation and in the confusion his 8th Division pushed Allanson off Hill Q.

After two days holding Chunuk Bair in the face of desperate Ottoman counter-attacks, the New Zealanders were now spent. By the evening of 9 August, the Otago Battalion had lost 17 officers and 309 men and the Wellington MRR was left with just 73 of the 183 with whom the unit had started. The Auckland Battalion, which had defended The Pinnacle, lost 12 officers and 308 men. Two British infantry battalions – 6th (Service) Battalion, The Loyal North Lancashire Regiment and 5th (Service) Battalion, The Duke of Edinburgh's (Wiltshire Regiment) – now moved up to replace the few surviving New Zealanders. The relief on the evening of 9 August commenced at 2000hrs but was not completed until 0200hrs on the morning of 10 August.

In the event, the New Zealanders could consider themselves fortunate to have escaped annihilation, for Kemal was massing his forces for a decisive offensive that would eliminate the threat presented by the enemy's possession of Chunuk Bair. Supported by massed artillery and machine-gun fire, the attack commenced at 0430hrs on 10 August. Ali Reza's 23rd and 24th regiments swept forward on the right, the 16th and 28th regiments on the left. On the 8th Division's right flank, the 9th Division's 25th Regiment and the 1st Battalion of the 33rd Regiment also joined in the assault. In total, Kemal committed about 16 battalions, approximately 6,000 men altogether, in a hammer blow, amounting to a human-wave attack achieved with almost complete surprise.

Wallingford now had ten machine guns in action at Chunuk Bair, six of them well forward, trained across the line of the Ottoman advance. The first two Ottoman waves charged into their fire and were slaughtered, but still they came on, wave after wave, even as ANZAC and Royal Navy artillery picked up the range, blasting great gaps in their ranks. Under this onslaught, the trenches holding Chunuk Bair were simply overwhelmed; the 6th Loyal North Lancashire and 5th Wiltshire functionally ceased to exist. The Ottomans continued to pour down the reverse slope, recapturing The Pinnacle. This left the British position at The Farm isolated and untenable; it was evacuated at dusk. The only strategic asset retained was The Apex, where in furious hand-to-hand combat the Auckland Battalion eventually stemmed the flow of the Ottoman tide.

Hamilton ascribed this outcome to 'lack of swift pressure from Suvla' (Hamilton 1920: II.86) but conceded that the Ottomans were ably led by commanders aware of Chunuk Bair's importance. Nevertheless, he remained

During World War I, many Ottoman troops used the German-manufactured 7.65mm Mauser M1903 bolt-action rifle; note how this model produced for the Ottoman Army has the settings for its sighting mechanism (incorporating a standard V-notch tangent rear sight adjustable in 50m increments from 100m to 2,000m) stamped with Farsi numerals. (© Royal Armouries PR.6539)

Australian troops stage a bayonet charge in this posed photograph. For the Allied troops clinging on in the Dardanelles, the final straw came on 29 November 1915 when the Ottomans commenced a massive bombardment against Lone Pine, utilizing howitzers that could be directly imported from Germany and Austria-Hungary now that the Berlin–Baghdad railway ran unhindered through occupied Serbia. The combination of high-explosive shells and their steep trajectory tore Lone Pine apart. Parts of the front literally ceased to exist, especially the northernmost areas where trenches were completely smashed in. It was a combination of these worsening environmental conditions, the tactical stalemate on the peninsula itself and the wider strategic picture that led to the British War Cabinet decision of 7 December to evacuate Gallipoli. Ironically, this withdrawal proved to be the best orchestrated operation of the campaign. The expeditionary force slipped away from Anzac Cove and Suvla Bay on 20 December, for the loss of two men wounded at Anzac Cove and not a single casualty at Suvla Bay. The MEF held the promontory at Cape Helles until shortly before 0400hrs on 9 January 1916, when its abandoned ammunition-dumps were detonated; not a casualty had been sustained, and by dawn not a man was left ashore. (British Official/Buyenlarge/Getty Images)

boundlessly optimistic about the ultimate outcome of the campaign. Ottoman casualties were enormous, but Kemal's gambit had succeeded. In five days of fighting, British and Imperial troops had failed to break out of the Ottoman defensive cordon and had lost one-third of their force; 12,500 from a total of 37,000 deployed.

Was the struggle for Chunuk Bair the crux of the campaign, as some accounts would have it? Hamilton certainly believed so (Hamilton 1920: II.205). In retrospect, it is likely that even if Chunuk Bair could have been held – a doubtful proposition – it would not have delivered the decisive blow either to Ottoman morale or to the overall Ottoman strategic advantage necessary for an Entente victory. No guns could have operated on the summit with Ottoman troops so close and above on Hill 971, while even if they could have, indirect fire on the Narrows or the roads linking the peninsula with Constantinople could not have stopped the flow of men and supplies south to Cape Helles, especially at night. Nor could artillery on Chunuk Bair have reduced the Ottoman forts screening the entrance to the Dardanelles, the main obstacle to the Entente fleet's passage through the Narrows.

In his after-action report, Kemal concluded that after being driven off Sari Bair the enemy had shot their bolt and could not mount another serious offensive at Gallipoli. This assessment was premature, for Hamilton was stubbornly convinced he could still bring the campaign to a successful conclusion. He advised Lord Kitchener that in order to make any further progress at Gallipoli, substantial reinforcements would have to be sent. Prospects for a quick victory by *coup de main* had by now completely evaporated: 'It has become a question of who can slog longest and hardest' (Hamilton 1920: II.117).

Beersheba

31 October 1917

BACKGROUND TO BATTLE

Although the Allies had wrested the strategic initiative from the Ottomans by the end of 1916, further Allied advance was limited by the grindingly slow projection of railway and water-pipeline infrastructure across the desert and it was not until 21 December 1916 that significant progress was made with the capture of El Arish. Lieutenant-General Chauvel was then tasked with taking the village of Magdhaba, which was captured on 23 December. The next Allied target was the village of Rafa, defended by the Ottoman Army's 31st Regiment. Lieutenant-General Sir Archibald James Murray, GOC Egyptian Expeditionary Force (EEF), assigned the task of capturing this locale to Chauvel's ANZAC Mounted Division, now composed of the 1st ALH Brigade (1st–4th ALH regiments), 3rd ALH Brigade (8th–11th ALH regiments) and the NZMR Brigade, accompanied by the Imperial Camel Corps (composed of two Australian battalions, one British battalion and a mixed Australian/New Zealand battalion) and the British 5th Mounted Brigade. Rafa was approached and surrounded on 9 January 1917, but the Ottoman garrison stubbornly held out until the NZMR Brigade stormed the key Ottoman redoubt on Hill 255. This unhinged the defensive line and the village fell, Allied forces taking 1,434 prisoners.

After this string of successes, Lieutenant-General Charles Macpherson Dobell, commander of Eastern Force, was confident that the Egyptian Expeditionary Force could capture the town of Gaza, which anchored the Ottoman defensive line across the Sinai barring Allied penetration into Palestine, by using enveloping tactics similar to those employed at Magdhaba and Rafa, only on a much grander scale. The cameleers and horsemen of Chetwode's Desert Mounted Corps, supported by a British infantry brigade,

This cigarette card depicts Lieutenant-General Sir Archibald James Murray, GOC Egyptian Expeditionary Force (EEF). After the failure of his offensives in the first and second battles of Gaza, Murray was succeeded by Lieutenant-General Sir Edmund Henry Hynman 'Bull' Allenby. (Print Collector/ Getty Images)

would sweep around behind the town, surrounding it and establishing an outer screen that would repel any attempts to relieve the garrison. The main assault would be undertaken by infantry of the 52nd, 53rd and 54th divisions, supported by two field-artillery brigades and an ad hoc battery of heavy artillery. This was by far the largest force mobilized by the EEF for a single operation, which meant a correspondingly heavy strain on the supply chain. The attackers could be supplied with food, water and ammunition for 24 hours at most. If they did not capture Gaza and its wells by nightfall they would have to withdraw to their jumping-off points.

The Allied offensive commenced when the DMC set out to encircle Gaza under cover of darkness early on the morning of 26 March. The ANZAC Mounted Division and Imperial Mounted Division easily succeeded in outflanking and isolating the town, cutting it off from communication or support from Huj to the north-east and Beersheba to the south-east. The main assault on Gaza did not go to plan, however. The start of the first phase of the Allied infantry attack, on the high ground of Ali Muntar, was delayed from 0800hrs until midday by a combination of dense fog, poor staff work and confusion among the divisional and brigade commanders. The British artillery bombardment was ineffective and the attacking infantry, advancing with little cover for much of the way, were met by a hail of Ottoman artillery, machine-gun and rifle fire. The 53rd Division suffered heavy losses and the assault quickly bogged down.

At 1300hrs, Chetwode ordered the ANZAC Mounted Division to attack Gaza from the north, commencing at 1600hrs. Jumping-off 20 minutes early, the ANZACs swiftly overwhelmed the thin Ottoman defences on the northern outskirts of the town. Resistance stiffened as the attackers entered the more built-up suburbs, where the buildings were intersected with cactus hedges. One Ottoman counter-attack against an advanced NZMR Brigade detachment was broken up when men of the 7th ALH broke through the prickly pear surrounding the neighbourhood. A trooper knelt down in the open while an officer levelled a Hotchkiss machine gun over his shoulder and blazed away at the advancing Ottomans, who were mown down or dispersed under the added crossfire of the New Zealanders.

Meanwhile, a squadron of the Canterbury MRR reached Ali Muntar and joined in the final battle to clear it. By 1630hrs, soldiers of the 53rd Division were linking up with the ANZACs in the streets of Gaza, as the remnants of the Ottoman garrison prepared to make a final stand or fled for their lives in the failing light. With dusk falling, the commander of the garrison advised his German superior, Oberst Friedrich Kress von Kressenstein, that the defence of Gaza was hopelessly compromised. Faced by certain defeat, Kress ordered the Ottoman reinforcements marching towards Gaza to halt, and authorized the ranking German officer in the town to surrender. At that moment, however, Kress's forces were reprieved, for Dobell had already ordered Allied forces to withdraw from Gaza. Alarmed by the reports of Ottoman reinforcements converging on the town, Dobell and Chetwode were not confident they could consolidate their gains sufficiently to hold off an Ottoman counter-attack either that night or the next day with a force short of food, water and ammunition.

The Allies suffered 3,967 casualties, the Ottomans 2,447. Undaunted, Murray made preparations for an immediate second attempt to take Gaza. This second battle commenced on 17 April. When the main assault went in two days later, despite the support of naval gunfire, poison gas and even tanks, the attacking British infantry were decimated by Ottoman artillery, machine-gun and rifle fire. On this occasion, well-coordinated Ottoman infantry, cavalry and artillery succeeded in neutralizing the DMC's efforts to outflank Gaza. The butcher's bill was high: 6,444 Allied casualties in total, nearly three times the toll on the Ottomans. This defeat cost Murray his post as commander of the EEF. He was replaced by Lieutenant-General Sir Edmund Henry Hynman 'Bull' Allenby on 29 June.

Allenby took his time in drafting an ambitious plan to take Gaza and break through the Ottoman line (now defended by the Ottoman Seventh and Eighth armies) into southern Palestine. He reorganized his infantry into two corps, XX and XXI, but as a career cavalryman, his primary intent lay in maximizing his advantage in mobility. This time, the main thrust would be directed not at Gaza on the coast but against Beersheba at the other end of the Ottoman line. While XXI Corps attacked the outer defences of Gaza to pin down the garrison and hold Ottoman attention, Beersheba would be stormed by the DMC (now the Desert Mounted Corps) and XX Corps. The DMC would subsequently move westwards to take Huj beyond Gaza, cutting off the line of retreat for those Ottoman units pinned down along the Gaza–Beersheba axis by XX and XXI corps. Allenby did not intend just to break through the Ottoman line – he wanted to destroy the two armies defending it.

On the afternoon of 28 October 1917, the regiments of the DMC began their march on Beersheba, moving largely at night to minimize the effects of the desert heat and avoid observation by enemy aircraft. On the evening of 30 October the Allied regiments moved into their positions around Beersheba, carefully remaining hidden in the surrounding wadis to prevent detection.

A veteran of the Second Anglo-Boer War and Gallipoli, Major-General Harry Chauvel, who had assumed command of the newly formed Anzac Mounted Division on 16 March 1916, won his spurs in the Sinai during the battle of Romani, beating back an Ottoman offensive that commenced on 3 August 1916. After the Ottomans drove in the outlying ALH units, Chauvel ordered the 1st ALH Brigade to close ranks with the NZMR Brigade to establish a firm defensive line, then personally brought the 2nd and 3rd ALH Brigades in from the flanks, funnelling the Ottomans into an area covered by British artillery. In the aftermath, Chauvel forced his weary troopers to keep the enemy on the run, pushing them back east towards Katia and El Arish. This Allied victory at Romani ended the Ottoman threat to the Suez Canal. (John Frost Newspapers/Alamy Stock Photo)

MAP KEY

1 Early morning: After a wide flanking manoeuvre through the desert that exhausts all supplies of water, Chauvel establishes his command headquarters about 6km south-east of Beersheba on the height of Khashm Zanna.

2 Early morning: The NZMR Brigade and the 1st, 5th and 7th ALH regiments push north-east of Beersheba to cut the road to Hebron.

3 Early morning: The 53rd Infantry Division swings north-west to block the road and rail line to Gaza, cutting the garrison at Beersheba off from reinforcement.

4 0555hrs: Covered by artillery fire, the 60th and 74th Infantry divisions advance on Beersheba to pin its Ottoman defenders – the 81st, 67th and 48th Infantry regiments – on the town's western flank.

5 0630hrs: The Ottoman 3rd Cavalry Division moves to block the encircling enemy cavalry north-east of Beersheba.

6 0700hrs: The Ottoman reserve – two battalions of the 24th Infantry Regiment – is deployed to cover the exposed approach to Beersheba on its eastern flank.

7 c.1300hrs: After a four-hour fight, the Ottoman outpost at Tel el-Sakaty falls to ALH units.

8 c.1500hrs: After nearly six hours of fighting, the Ottoman outpost at Tel el-Saba falls to the NZMR Brigade.

9 1600hrs: With the situation becoming hopeless, İsmet orders the wells in Beersheba destroyed and all units of the garrison still capable of doing so to disengage and seek to escape north through the thin cavalry screen established by the 1st ALH.

10 1630hrs: With the water situation critical, the 4th and 12th ALH regiments stage a mounted charge in order to take Beersheba by storm. The ALH break through the Ottoman lines and successfully occupy the town, taking its vital wells intact.

Battlefield environment

If Beersheba fell, the Ottoman defensive line would be unhinged, Gaza outflanked, and the road through Hebron to Jerusalem would be opened. It was a priceless strategic asset for another reason: the town contained at least 17 wells, without which it would be impossible to continue any advance north out of the Negev. Indeed, the greatest challenge to operational planning of the Beersheba offensive was finding sources of water in the region sufficient to support the number of mounted troops required to take the town. Initial intelligence reports assumed there were none, other than at Esani, which was too far to the west to be of any use for a surprise attack. Having studied the 19th-century records of the Palestine Exploration Fund and questioned indigenous Arabs, however, Chauvel knew that the larger ancient towns in the area to the south and south-west of Beersheba must have had water supplies at some point. At Asluj, about 50km from Beersheba, the old wells were found, and a fortnight's work rendered them viable. This made the Beersheba operation feasible, but only barely; after watering at Asluj, it would be 48 hours before horses could drink water again, and then only if the wells at Beersheba could be taken. If the town could not be stormed at the first assault, the DMC would not be capable of maintaining a siege. Even assuming Beersheba was successfully stormed, if the garrison destroyed the wells before they could be seized, the DMC could not hold the town. In either scenario, the DMC would be forced into a withdrawal that would push men and mounts beyond physical endurance. In many ways, therefore, the Beersheba operation was an all-or-nothing gamble.

Ottoman military authorities had evacuated the civilian population of Beersheba. The town lay in a shallow valley, the Wadi Saba, running east to west: with the surrounding hills, it formed a natural impediment to north–south movement. The main avenues of approach into the town were the six roads and tracks radiating out from its centre, evenly distributed with three to the north and three to the south of the Wadi Saba. Ottoman defence lines surrounding Beersheba included redoubts dug-in to the heights of the hills north and south of the town overlooking the approaches, and an interlacing system of trench lines on level ground, from which soldiers could fire either in prone positions from the shallow forward trenches or standing within the deeper rear trenches. The trenches incorporated arrowhead-shaped projections, to allow machine-gunners at the tip to fire forward and enfilade to the flanks. These were supported by artillery batteries positioned to their rear.

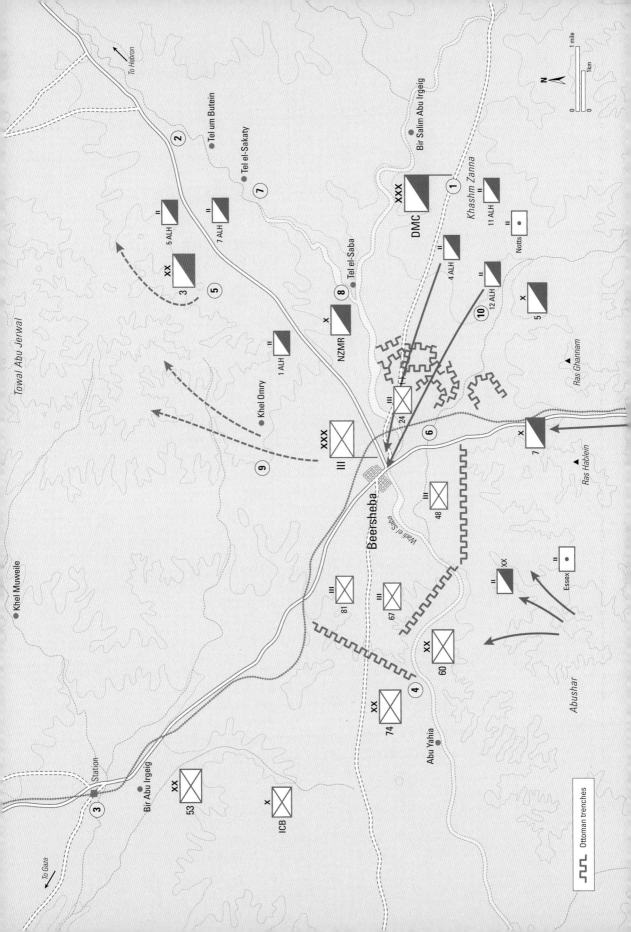

To Hebron

Tel um Butein

Tel el-Sakaty

② ⑦

5 ALH
7 ALH

XX
3

⑤

1 ALH

NZMR

Tel el-Saba

⑧

Khel Omry

III
XXX

⑨

Towal Abu Jerwal

Khel Muweile

Beersheba

Wadi el-Saba

③

Bir Abu Irgeig

Station

To Gaza

53

ICB

74

60

④

Abu Yahia

67

81

48

III

⑥

7

Essex

Ras Hablein

Ras Ghannam

Abushar

5

12 ALH

⑩

4 ALH

Notts

11 ALH

①

Khashm Zanna

DMC
XXX

Bir Salim Abu Irgeig

N

1 mile
1km
0

Ottoman trenches

Born in Motueka, New Zealand, on 21 June 1868, Edward Walter Clervaux Chaytor served as a captain in the Third New Zealand Contingent and subsequently as a lieutenant-colonel in the Eighth New Zealand Contingent during the Second Anglo-Boer War. After serving at Gallipoli, he took command of the NZMR Brigade of the Egyptian Expeditionary Force (EEF) in the Sinai. In April 1917 Chaytor was promoted to major-general and succeeded Australian Major-General Henry George 'Harry' Chauvel in command of the Australian and New Zealand Mounted Division, becoming the only New Zealander to command an ANZAC force at this level. Seeing action in all the major battles of the Sinai campaign, from Katia to Beersheba, in 1918 Chaytor was placed in command of a composite unit dubbed Chaytor's Force, which fought a series of bitterly contested actions in the Transjordan to focus Ottoman attention away from the build-up to the main EEF offensive at Megiddo. The climax of this campaign was the capture of Amman on 25 September 1918. (FLHC 220C/Alamy Stock Photo)

INTO COMBAT

Early on the morning of 31 October, Chauvel established his command headquarters about 6km south-east of Beersheba on a high hill called Khashm Zanna, which gave good views of the battlefield. From here he ordered Chaytor's ANZAC Mounted Division to close the Beersheba road at Sakaty, almost 10km north-east of the town, in order to prevent Ottoman reinforcements from arriving and also to cut off any Ottoman escape from Beersheba.

The three infantry divisions of XX Corps would attack the main Ottoman defences on the western and south-western outskirts of Beersheba to fix the enemy's attention on this sector. The Yeomanry Mounted Division would tie-in with the XX Corps cavalry, which was screening their own corps' right flank. Once the Ottomans had committed their reserves to the western side of the town, the Australian Mounted Division (3rd and 4th ALH brigades and British 5th Mounted Brigade) would ride in a wide arc to the relatively open flank south-east of Beersheba in order to storm the town from the rear. The assault would commence at 0555hrs, giving Chauvel about 11 hours of daylight in which to execute his plan.

In order to assume control of the eastern outskirts of Beersheba, the ANZAC and Australian mounted divisions first had to capture two redoubts on outlying hilltops, Tel el-Sakaty and Tel el-Saba. Tel el-Sakaty was taken at about 1300hrs after a four-hour fight. Tel el-Saba, which had been allocated to the NZMR Brigade, proved an even tougher nut to crack. The attack commenced just after 0900hrs and the Ottoman defenders – a battalion of the 48th Regiment and a machine-gun company – held out until close to 1500hrs when the Auckland MRR, with the Canterbury MRR on its right and the 1st ALH Regiment to its left, was able to storm the heights. Using the protection of a wadi, with a battery of light field guns and machine guns providing covering fire, the Auckland MRR rushed the position, which finally fell, conceding control of the approaches from Jerusalem and Hebron and, critically, eliminating the possibility of Ottoman enfilading fire on the approaches to Beersheba along the roads from both the east and the plain in the south, thus opening up the potential for an Allied assault on the town from those directions.

Beersheba had begun to receive artillery fire at 0555hrs, and by 0745hrs Colonel Mustafa İsmet Bey was aware of the scale of the attack as cavalry began to sweep around his lightly defended eastern flank. Shortly thereafter, he deployed the two battalions of the 24th Regiment to establish hasty defensive positions directly east of the town, and at 0900hrs he ordered the 3rd Cavalry Division to block the encircling enemy cavalry north-east of Beersheba. Esat reported at 1020hrs that the enemy cavalry attack was much stronger than expected. Along the line fighting was particularly heavy in the 67th Regiment's sector.

By early afternoon, after the fall of Tel el-Sakaty and Tel el-Saba, it was obvious to İsmet, who had been directing the battle on his own recognizance since 1200hrs after Brigadier-General Mustafa Fevzi Çakmak was cut off from news from Beersheba when the telegraph line was cut, that encirclement was all but certain. At 1600hrs he ordered the surviving elements of III Corps to

FAR LEFT
Ottoman Army colour-bearers.
This standard was presented
to the defenders of Gaza after
their victory in the first battle
on 26 March 1917. (Library of
Congress)

LEFT
An Ottoman Army divisional
commander inspects
defensive positions near
Gaza, 1917. Allenby's
Ottoman and German
antagonists anticipated any
forthcoming Allied offensive
would be focused against
Gaza, accompanied by a
feint against Beersheba.
The defenders' assumptions
were apparently confirmed
on 10 October when an
intelligence bonanza
dropped into their laps. In
fact, this was a bluff, the
'lost haversack episode'
hatched by Major Richard
Meinertzhagen. These false
operational documents
played into the intelligence
estimates of the Ottoman
and German staff officers.
Accordingly, the Eighth Army
shifted three infantry divisions
to the Gaza end of the line.
Brigadier-General Mustafa
Fevzi Çakmak's Seventh Army
was stationed to hold the
Ottoman left, which was
anchored at Beersheba,
defended by Colonel Mustafa
İsmet Bey's III Corps: its 27th
Division occupied trenches
on the eastern and southern
sides of Beersheba, with
the 81st, 67th and 48th
regiments, in line from north
to south and east, defending
a 12km line. Each regiment
had a battalion in immediate
reserve and artillery and
machine guns were tied into
the defensive plan. İsmet
kept Colonel Esat Pasha's
two-regiment 3rd Cavalry
Division deployed in the high
ground north-east of the
town, and two battalions of
the 24th Regiment in general
reserve. (ullstein bild/ullstein
bild via Getty Images)

break out to the north. German pioneers attached to the garrison commenced preparations to destroy the town's infrastructure before it could fall into Allied hands. Critically, this included the wells. The loss of these would render the capture of Beersheba moot, for without water, the town could not support occupation by the DMC, let alone serve as the jumping-off point for subsequent Allied offensive operations.

With only a few hours of daylight remaining, and both horses and men desperately in need of water, at 1600hrs Chauvel called for the commanders of the Yeomanry and Australian divisions to meet with him. Briefing the situation to his subordinates, Chauvel pointed out that Beersheba was now effectively isolated, but that taking the town itself would require a final advance across several kilometres of open ground covered by Ottoman machine-gun and artillery fire, and would have to be accomplished before sundown at 1650hrs. The commanding officer of the 4th ALH Brigade, Brigadier-General William Grant, straightaway stepped forward and stated that he could seize the town with a cavalry charge. He had no doctrinal or experiential basis on which to make this assertion, however; the ALH was a mounted-infantry force that had neither trained for nor conducted a cavalry charge in its history, and was not even equipped to do so, lacking sabres. Brigadier-General Percy Desmond Fitzgerald of the Yeomanry Division immediately registered disagreement and requested that his troops be allowed to conduct the attack, since they were armed with sabres. The Yeomanry were several kilometres further south, however, stationed to the rear of the 4th ALH Brigade. It would take longer for the British troops to reach the start line, and it might be twilight before they could be committed to action. After weighing his options for a moment, Chauvel turned to Major-General Sir Henry West Hodgson, GOC Australian Mounted Division, and ordered, 'Put Grant straight at it.'

By 1630hrs the two leading regiments of the 4th ALH Brigade – Lieutenant-Colonel Murray William James Bourchier's 4th (Victoria) and Lieutenant-Colonel Donald Cameron's 12th (New South Wales);

Mustafa İsmet İnönü

Born in Smyrna (modern-day İzmir, Turkey) on 24 September 1884, Mustafa İsmet received a military education. A member of the Committee of Union and Progress, he participated in the march on Constantinople to depose Sultan Abdul Hamid II in 1909. His career unscathed, he fought in Yemen in 1911 and during the First Balkan War at the first and second battles of Çatalca in 1912.

Promoted to lieutenant-colonel on 29 November 1914, İsmet became chief of staff of the Second Army on 9 October 1915, being promoted to colonel on 14 December 1915. While serving as a corps commander on the Caucasian Front he began a lifelong military and political partnership with Mustafa Kemal (Atatürk). On 20 June 1917, İsmet was appointed commander of III Corps in Palestine. Wounded during the battle of Megiddo in 1918, İsmet was recalled to Constantinople,

being appointed Undersecretary of the Ministry of War on 24 October.

Repudiating Allied occupation and dictation to a puppet Ottoman regime, İsmet escaped from Constantinople and in August 1920, was appointed the first Chief of the General Staff of the Turkish Armed Forces and to command of the critical Western Front of the Army of the GNA. Fighting to hold back a Greek invasion, İsmet was victorious at the battles of First and Second İnönü in early 1921.

Following the Turkish victory in September 1922, İsmet was appointed to lead the Turkish delegation that negotiated the July 1923 Treaty of Lausanne formally recognizing Turkish sovereignty. İnönü served as prime minister during 1925–37 and succeeded Atatürk as president during 1938–50. He died on 25 December 1973 at the age of 89.

Mustafa İsmet, photographed after returning with the rank of captain from his first combat tour in the Yemen. His unsuccessful defence of Beersheba and its all-important wells on 31 October 1917 as the colonel commanding the Ottoman III Corps was subsequently subject to criticism by his German superior at Eighth Army headquarters, Oberst Friedrich Kress von Kressenstein, but the fact İsmet was able to hold out almost until nightfall, and escape with a considerable percentage of his men before the town fell, did reflect to his credit. (Historic Collection/ Alamy Stock Photo)

approximately 1,000 men in total, 500 in each regiment – were assembled at their jumping-off points behind rising ground approximately 7km south-east of Beersheba. The 11th (Queensland) ALH Regiment was standing close by in reserve. The gradual slope of the terrain to the south of Beersheba provided little or no cover to an attacking force, which would have to traverse several kilometres of open ground before reaching the town. Owing to Ottoman deficiencies in supply, however, barbed wire had not been strung all the way around the town and the defences were incomplete on the southern and south-eastern approaches, a fact confirmed by British and Australian aerial reconnaissance.

Over the first kilometre the troopers advanced at a walk and slow trot, with the 4th ALH on the right, the 12th ALH on the left. Within each regiment, the troopers were riding in a traditional squadron frontage, two squadrons wide and three lines deep, a frontage of about 200 men with the remainder in depth, 300yd (275m) between each squadron. The troopers of the brigade immediately opened their intervals to about 5m to prevent mass casualties from artillery or machine-gun fire. Over the next 2km the two lines accelerated to a canter. Once the Australians began to take incoming fire, they broke into a full gallop and charged hell for leather.

Under normal circumstance, a charge by bayonet-wielding light horsemen across several kilometres of open ground against entrenched infantry supported by artillery, machine guns and aircraft would be tantamount to suicide. The defenders, however, never anticipated that the ALH would ride straight over the top of them and on into the town. Ironically, Ottoman officers, having correctly identified the advancing horsemen as mounted infantry, issued instructions to hold fire until the ALH reached the trenches and dismounted to start the fight. Counting on the Australians to attack on foot, the Ottoman defenders set their sights to 1,600m. As the charge gained momentum and speed, however, the Ottoman troops lost their composure

Henry George 'Harry' Chauvel

Henry George Chauvel was born in Tabulam, New South Wales, on 16 April 1865. In 1886, he was commissioned as a second lieutenant in the Upper Clarence Light Horse. Posted to England for Queen Victoria's Diamond Jubilee in 1897, he became a staff officer at headquarters, Queensland Defence Force, upon returning to Australia. During the Second Anglo-Boer War, Chauvel participated in relieving the siege of Kimberley, the capture of Pretoria and the battle of Diamond Hill. He was promoted to the brevet rank of lieutenant-colonel in December 1902, and to colonel in 1913.

Upon the outbreak of World War I, Chauvel assumed command of the AIF's 1st ALH Brigade. On 9 July, he was promoted to brigadier-general, and on 6 November to major-general and command of the 1st Division. Chauvel assumed command of the newly formed ANZAC Mounted Division on 16 March 1916. After playing a key role in the Allied victory at the battle of Romani (3–5 August), Chauvel enhanced his status with additional victories at the battles of Magdhaba (23 December 1916) and Rafa (9 January 1917). Having participated in the two defeats at Gaza (26 March and 17–19 April), Chauvel succeeded to command of the Desert Column, later the Desert Mounted Corps, which played a critical role in the decisive battles of Beersheba (31 October 1917) and Megiddo (19–25 September 1918).

In 1919, Chauvel was appointed Inspector General, the Australian Army's most senior post, and was concurrently Chief of the General Staff from 1923 until his retirement in 1930. During World War II, he was recalled to duty as Inspector in Chief of the Volunteer Defence Corps, in which capacity he served until his death on 4 March 1945.

and forgot to adjust the sights on their weapons. Accordingly, they mostly fired high, and it was afterwards found that the sights of their rifles were never lowered below 800m. In addition, the supporting British artillery batteries were tasked with identifying and neutralizing the Ottoman machine guns, and soon silenced most of them with accurate salvos. By contrast, Ottoman artillery was unable to estimate the pace of the ALH charge and its shells all went over the heads of the advancing troops. Although two German aircraft attacked the ALH from above, firing machine guns and dropping bombs, they also failed to have much impact; the horses were too spread out and the bombs exploded harmlessly between the widely spaced lines of horses.

Nevertheless, casualties were inevitable, men and mounts being cut down by bullets and shrapnel. Horses with no riders kept galloping, saddles splashed with blood. Dismounted troopers ran to take shelter behind dead horses, the only cover on the open plain. Far from being some mad dash, however, the ALH action was staged and tightly coordinated. The first rank of squadrons in the regiments jumped the first line of Ottoman trenches and broke into the bivouac area in the rear before dismounting and clearing the reserve and support trenches. The second rank of squadrons also jumped the first line of trenches, then dismounted to storm them from the rear. The third rank of squadrons dismounted in front of the first line of trenches to support the assault by the second rank. Only when the trenches had been secured did the ALH remount and press on to Beersheba.

Instances of personal courage abounded. After charging most of the way to the Ottoman lines, Second Anglo-Boer War veteran Major Cuthbert Murchison Fetherstonhaugh of the 12th ALH Regiment had his horse shot out from under him just 40m short of the first Ottoman trench. Covering the rest of the distance on foot he survived a hail of bullets and leapt in among the defenders, emptying his revolver into the enemy and holding his ground until being shot through both legs. For his courage under fire, he would be

The ALH charge at Beersheba

Australian view: It is late afternoon at the end of a day full of fighting. The ANZAC spearheads of the British Army are victorious, but their victory will count for naught if they cannot seize the vital wells of Beersheba before they are demolished by the withdrawing enemy. With stakes this high, the gamble of charging the Ottoman trenches protecting Beersheba is a risk that has to be taken. In this perspective, a mounted trooper of the second wave can make out the key features of the town, where smoke is rising, both from artillery strikes and from the defenders' attempts to destroy vital infrastructure. Riding at full gallop across the arid terrain, he is caught up in the agony and exhilaration of the charge; men shot out of the saddle; horses still determinedly dashing on towards the enemy without riders. He can see the troopers of the first wave have already breached the Ottoman front line, some by leaping their horses over the trenches; in moments, it will be his turn.

Ottoman view: Ottoman infantry in the reserve trenches, charged with covering the retreat of the garrison as it pulls out of Beersheba and buying enough time for the demolition crews to complete their work, witness their comrades in the front line being overrun by the Australian charge. Some are breaking and, abandoning the shelter of their trenches, are fleeing for the rear – the worst option, as men on foot on open ground make themselves easy prey for their mounted assailants. Others hunker down and attempt to hold their ground; some thrust upwards with their bayonets as the ALH troopers leap over them, tearing out the exposed bellies of the horses. Most are armed with Mauser M1890 bolt-action rifles, while a machine-gun crew manning their water-cooled, tripod-mounted MG 09 desperately lays down a suppressing fire. But most of these shots go harmlessly high and over the heads of the oncoming enemy; within moments, it will be their turn to take the full impact of the charge.

awarded the Distinguished Service Order. Having reached the first Ottoman trench, Quartermaster Sergeant Alfred Richard Townsend and 17-year-old Sergeant Harry Harvison Peard took it upon themselves to eliminate an Ottoman redoubt situated a few hundred metres to the west of the ALH advance. Making their way through the trenches, the two NCOs shot ten of the enemy, captured two more and routed the remainder, thus silencing the enfilading fire. As their citation for the Distinguished Conduct Medal concluded, this clearance of the redoubt allowed the ALH clear passage to the town, saving the lives of many Allied soldiers.

Although the limited number of entrances to Beersheba and its narrow streets temporarily checked the headlong ALH advance, the horsemen swiftly came to terms with the town's layout, and from that moment, falling beams from fired buildings, exploding magazines and hidden snipers were unable to check their race through the two available streets that were wide enough for two men to ride abreast. The ALH reached the centre of the town at about 1830hrs, ending the battle. Demolition of the wells by the Germans was prevented by the audacity of the charge, which caught the defenders within the town completely off-guard. With the sources of water secured, men and mounts of the ALH could at last slake their desperate thirst.

The ALH action at Beersheba was the largest mounted charge by Western cavalry forces during World War I, both unprecedented and subsequently unsurpassed in any other theatre in its scale and in terms of its significance. Remarkably, only 31 troopers of the ALH had been killed, among them First Anglo-Boer War veteran and Victoria Cross recipient Lieutenant-Colonel Leslie Cecil Maygar, and 36 wounded; 44 horses were killed, many having received terrible injuries when the Ottomans thrust their bayonets upwards into the horses' bellies as the ALH hurdled the trenches. Ottoman casualties

Ottoman troops in the Sinai. The *Exerzier-Reglement für die Infanterie*, the pre-war German military manual around which the Ottoman Army of World War I was moulded, assured that men in such a defensive line, especially if armed as depicted with machine guns, were effectively invulnerable to the threat of a mounted charge. At Beersheba, the ALH proved such assumptions wrong. (Library of Congress)

ABOVE LEFT
Ottoman cavalry, staging a charge west of Beersheba. As with its ANZAC counterpart, the cavalry was the elite arm of the Ottoman Army. Reflecting the consistently inferior Ottoman logistical situation, however, lack of fodder and good horses placed the cavalry at a distinct disadvantage by the time of the Beersheba campaign. Quantitatively, they were outnumbered by about 6.5:1. Qualitatively, Ottoman mounts were no match for the better fed and cared for DMC 'Walers'. (Library of Congress)

ABOVE RIGHT
Ottoman camel troops on the march in the Sinai Peninsula. Given the challenging climate and terrain, both sides made extensive use of camels, the original 'ship of the desert', in both a combat role and to meet logistical needs. In the absence of viable roads and railways, and with water in critically short supply, keeping armies viable – let alone functional – was a constant challenge. (Library of Congress)

amounted to approximately 500 men killed, 2,000 men missing (1,947 were reported taken prisoner by the British) and 13 guns captured. The tally could have been much greater. İsmet's order to pull out of Beersheba before it was encircled ensured the survival of the Ottoman III Corps. The 3rd Cavalry Division, the only Ottoman cavalry division in Palestine, successfully broke through the porous Allied cavalry screens, while the 27th Division, although badly battered, survived the debacle intact as well.

Although Fevzi and İsmet successfully conducted a fighting withdrawal north from Beersheba, Gaza was now outflanked and threatened with encirclement. The Ottoman garrison had been subjected to an intense artillery and naval barrage since 27 October, including poison gas, and had been fighting bitterly to repulse the British ground assault since 2 November. The threat to the Ottoman rear forced Colonel Refet Bey to order the evacuation of Gaza under cover of night on 6/7 November, and the British occupied the abandoned town the next day.

While the Ottoman defensive line had been broken, Allenby had not trapped and destroyed the Ottoman Seventh and Eighth armies, which pulled back north to Jerusalem. The EEF set off in pursuit. Pushing into the famous orange-groves of Jaffa, on 14 November, the 800-strong NZMR Brigade encountered an Ottoman force of 1,500 men, supported by 18 machine guns and a battery of field artillery, entrenched on a ridge south of the village of Ayun Kara. The Auckland and Wellington MRRs attacked and the firefight that followed lasted more than three hours. The NZMR Brigade seized Ayun Kara, but the action resulted in the heaviest casualty list of the campaign: 44 killed and 141 wounded. The NZMR Brigade took Jaffa on 16 November, having covered the 105km from Beersheba in just five days.

Ottoman counter-attacks by the Seventh Army on 22 November and Eighth Army three days later were defeated. Allenby's offensive to seize Jerusalem began on 7 December, and early on the morning of 9 December the holy city was abandoned by the Ottomans, the 10th ALH Regiment being among the first EEF units to take possession. When Allenby made his formal entry into the city via the Jaffa Gate on 11 December he was escorted by a troop of the NZMR Brigade.

Analysis

The Ottoman victory at Gallipoli was the result of many factors. Perhaps first among these were the fatal flaws of Allied strategic goals themselves, which exhibited both overconfidence and under-planning. Fundamentally, the Allies did not possess an overwhelming advantage in manpower or *matériel* and were attacking prepared defensive positions on hostile terrain without the benefit of surprise. The only hope for success thus devolved upon the Ottoman enemy displaying low morale and poor leadership. Neither of those conditions applied. The British encountered enemy officers at company, battalion, regiment, division and corps level who were aggressive and skilled in the conduct of war. Ottoman field commanders consistently displayed an astute appreciation of the tactical situation, reacting with both flexibility and determination to each Allied initiative as it evolved. The organizational architecture of the Ottoman Army lent itself to the effective ability to cross-attach regiments and battalions. The triangular architecture of Ottoman infantry divisions proved highly flexible and enabled Ottoman commanders to concentrate forces effectively at the point of greatest enemy pressure, repeatedly detaching a regiment or battalion from one division and attaching it to another with no real loss of capability. Ottoman officers could rely upon their rank and file being both tenacious in defence and ferocious in the counter-attack. Thus, at no point during the struggle for Gallipoli were the Allies in a position to dominate their opponents either physically or psychologically. The architects of the campaign in Whitehall had drawn the wrong lessons from history. The Ottoman Empire had garnered its reputation as 'The Sick Man of Europe' from its inability to maintain its steadily shrinking perimeter over the past century; but the succession of defeats it suffered – at the hands of the Russians, Italians and insurgent former Balkan subjects – had occurred throughout the imperial periphery. It would be a different story once the Turkish heartland itself was under threat. Fighting on their own soil, in defence of their own capital, the Ottoman military at

This monument stands today at the peak of Chunuk Bair, the highest elevation attained by ANZAC forces during the Gallipoli campaign. The inscription reads simply: 'In honour of the soldiers of the New Zealand Expeditionary Force 8th August 1915: "From the Uttermost Ends of the Earth"'. (Author's Collection)

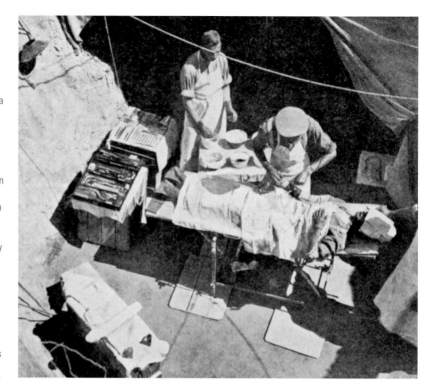

A surgeon removes a bullet from the arm of a wounded soldier at Gallipoli. MEF casualties over the course of the Gallipoli campaign are calculated at 132,175. Among the ANZACs, Australia lost 7,825 killed and 17,900 wounded for total casualties of 25,725;. New Zealand lost 2,445 killed and 4,752 wounded for total casualties of 7,197. Some units had been functionally decimated. Of the 477 men who landed with the 5th ALH Regiment, only 105 were left at the end of the campaign. The Canterbury MRR, which had arrived at Gallipoli with nearly 650 officers and men, evacuated only 28, having lost 118 killed in action or succumbed to disease, plus 45 missing and 443 hospitalized sick or wounded. Ottoman casualties on the Gallipoli peninsula from 25 April to 19 December 1915 are calculated at 190,463. Of the Ottoman rank and file, 56,145 were killed in combat, 18,746 succumbed in hospital (primarily of disease) and a further 8,307 were lost to weather-related incidents. (Universal History Archive/ Getty Images)

all levels was prepared to stand and fight for every metre of ground between Cape Helles and Constantinople.

The terms of the conflict reflected an Ottoman advantage at multiple levels. They held the heights, with the commensurate benefits of observation, repeatedly forcing the ANZACs at Gallipoli to launch their assaults uphill. This confronted Allied leadership with the necessity of choosing from two heavily compromised alternatives: either attack during the day, in direct line of enemy sight; or attack under cover of darkness, thereby risking loss of unit cohesion and failure to adhere to timetables. The inherent challenges to both of these alternatives were never overcome by the ANZACs. Ill and dehydrated even before the first shots were fired, ANZAC troops at Lone Pine and Chunuk Bair would be confronted with the challenge of undertaking the rigours of combat against a determined foe dug in on the high ground of rugged terrain. While the ANZACs would attack with great élan throughout the August offensives, and stubbornly cling to the gains they had succeeded in wresting from the enemy, the Ottomans in turn were equally tenacious in defence and determined on the counter-attack. Although the ANZACs were initially successful in achieving operational surprise at both Lone Pine and in the attempt to seize the heights of Sari Bair, this advantage swiftly dissipated in the grinding attrition of trench warfare and the dispersed nature of the fighting for control of Chunuk Bair. Decisively, even while aware of the additional threat imposed by the major Allied landings at Suvla Bay, Ottoman command at all levels refused to panic and never lost control of the strategic situation. Reinforcements were committed to the critical sectors, and officers – leading from the front if necessary – deployed their men first to stall and then to roll back the Allied advance.

The availability and quality of medical care was critical to the outcome at Gallipoli. Each Ottoman infantry division had an organic medical company as well as a field hospital. Every Ottoman army corps also had an assigned field hospital. Behind these forward facilities, there were 22 area hospitals in the towns of southern Thrace, with capacity for 11,080 beds, manned by 4,006 doctors, nurses and orderlies. Moreover, there were four Constantinople ferryboats converted for casualty evacuation as well as two hospital ships (*Akdeniz* and *Gülnihal*) with a combined additional 1,600 beds. By contrast, the rudimentary field dressing stations available to the ANZACs were swiftly overwhelmed by the number and severity of the cases pouring in from Lone Pine and Chunuk Bair, necessitating thousands of wounded and sick men to undertake the protracted and difficult process of evacuation by boat to offshore hospital ships and the long sojourn to convalescence in the Greek islands, Alexandria or Europe.

The role of geography was the hinge factor that determined the outcome of both the Gallipoli and Middle East campaigns. It is no coincidence that the wider the theatre of operations, the greater the progress made by Allied forces. The initial struggle for the Sinai was protracted because the front was narrow, the climate was brutal and the terrain inhospitable to man and beast. Massed frontal assaults against prepared Ottoman positions (e.g. the Second Battle of Gaza) proved costly failures in the Middle East for the same reason the Western Front was stalemated in France and Flanders; even when significantly outnumbered, infantry, properly dug in and supported by barbed wire to their front and artillery to their rear, had a decisive advantage over enemy forces advancing over open ground. The critical breakthrough at Beersheba was accomplished through the confluence of multiple Allied advantages in logistics, intelligence, and mobility. The aggregation of these tactical advantages created the context for a decisive strategic victory, accomplished through astute leadership and individual initiative.

Once the Ottoman line was finally destabilized at Beersheba, rendering the defences at Gaza redundant, the Allies were able to push into Palestine, which provided Allenby both a more forgiving environment (e.g. running water and fodder for his horses) in which to build up his force structure and wider room to manoeuvre, thus offering more options for the next phase of offensive operations. The cumulative effect of this trend culminated in the sudden and dramatic total collapse of the Ottoman force structure at the battle of Megiddo and subsequent sweeping Allied advance over the final few weeks of the war.

Freedom of movement thus emerges as the key to Allied victory. At Gallipoli, ANZAC cavalry units went into combat without their mounts,

The heir to the Ottoman throne and members of his staff visit the Gallipoli front, 1915. The Gallipoli campaign ended in a complete Ottoman strategic victory. Constantinople had been saved; Russia remained isolated; and the Central Powers had been gifted a huge fillip in morale and diplomatic prestige, had added a new partner in Bulgaria, had eliminated Serbia and now dominated the Balkans, tightening the Berlin–Constantinople axis. The Ottoman state had definitively arrested its apparently terminal decline, simultaneously repulsing the Allied offensive at Gallipoli and invasion of Mesopotamia, which culminated in the surrender of the besieged garrison at Kut al-Amara on 29 April 1916. Assumptions in Whitehall regarding the vulnerability of the Ottoman Empire and the benefits that could accrue from an early and easy victory had proved entirely inaccurate. For the ANZACs, the war would continue, along a much longer and harder road than anticipated. (Smith Collection/ Gado/Getty Images)

Ottoman infantry manning a front-line trench in the Sinai. The defensive pattern – note the arrowhead-shaped projection manned by a machine-gun crew, which could deliver enfilading fire to either flank – is typical of the configuration of the Ottoman trenches in Palestine. (Library of Congress)

for there was no possible way by which to maintain, let alone deploy, horses on the constricted beachheads and in the rough gullies of that landscape. Conversely, on the increasingly open ground of the Middle East, ANZAC cavalry could be utilized as intended, exploiting breaches, striking at and around the Ottoman flanks, and pouring into the rear areas, disrupting communications, raiding stores and cutting off retreats. In one of the last great cavalry campaigns of history, the ANZAC horsemen served as a force multiplier, each tactical victory exponentially strengthening the Allied strategic position and weakening that of the Ottomans.

The final factor at play in determining how the clash between ANZAC and Ottoman combatants would be resolved was the ultimate force potential of their respective empires far behind the front lines. The simple fact was that the Allies had greater resources – in manpower, raw materials, industrial might and financial reserves – than the Central Powers. This was not immediately deterministic, however, and could not compensate for the strategic blunders of the Gallipoli campaign (or in Mesopotamia, which culminated in the debacle at Kut al-Amara on 29 April 1916). Over time, the pressure told as Allied mobilization for total war moved into high gear.

In Palestine, poor diet and inadequate clothing undermined the immune systems of the Ottoman soldiers and contributed to an increase in exposure to diseases such as dysentery, typhus and malaria. It is estimated that about 400,000 Ottoman troops died from contagious diseases during World War I, about 13 per cent of the 2,850,000 men who enlisted. Given the worsening conditions of service, desertion became an increasingly endemic reality for Ottoman policy-makers as World War I entered its final phase. The estimated 500,000 Ottoman deserters amounted to another 17 per cent of the total number of men enlisted during the war. Many deserters congregated in bands that roamed behind the lines, placing additional stress on the gendarmerie tasked with maintaining order. The Ottoman ranks were therefore already significantly thinned out even before the Allies landed their final decisive blows against their outgunned, malnourished and ill-clad foes.

Aftermath

Having taken the propaganda prize of Jerusalem, and smashed a major Ottoman counter-attack during 27–29 December 1917, the EEF spent the first three months of 1918 preparing for a large-scale offensive against the Ottoman forces now holding a front line anchored to the east on the Dead Sea and to the west on the Mediterranean Sea. In February and early March 1918 the EEF carried out a series of local attacks, capturing Jericho on 21 February and establishing a new front line on the coastal plain north of the Auja River.

An Australian horseman – Trooper William Henry Nicholls of Leichhardt, Sydney, who was killed on 7 May 1918 in an Ottoman air raid on Jericho two hours after this photograph was taken – and his mount. During World War I, about 139,000 'Walers' (as the horses of the ALH were known) were transported overseas from outback stations. By the spring of 1918, the ALH and the NZMR Brigade constituted over one-half of all horsed cavalry in the EEF. Other than divisional squadrons, all horsed cavalry in the EEF were placed under the command of Lieutenant-General Chauvel of the Desert Mounted Corps. This unit continued to expand until it included more than 28,000 horsemen, making it the largest tactical cavalry force in Western history ever to serve under a single commander. (The State Library of New South Wales)

Ottoman infantry defending rocky terrain north of Jerusalem. From an Ottoman point of view, the operational and tactical situation in Palestine in the summer of 1918 could only be described as desperate, and Sultan Mehmet VI (r. 1918–22) asked that Kemal be reappointed to command the Seventh Army. Enver Pasha relented and Kemal took command of the army on 7 August. The Seventh Army was one of three field armies assigned to the newly created Yıldırım Army Group in Palestine, which was now under the command of Kemal's superior at Gallipoli, Liman von Sanders, who had been appointed a field marshal (*Müşir*), the highest ranking officer in the Ottoman Army. From September, Ottoman soldiers began to surrender by the thousands; Chaytor's command alone took 10,300 prisoners and 57 guns at a cost of just 139 casualties. It was symptomatic of how comprehensive the Ottoman collapse was becoming that some Turkish troops offered to surrender on condition their captors protect them from the marauding Arabs threatening to kill them. Those still attempting to flee were ridden down by Allied horsemen or strafed and bombed by Allied aircraft. (Library of Congress)

Although Allied forces were unable to take and hold bridgeheads on the Ottoman-controlled east bank of the Jordan River in two major raids during March and April 1918, at the strategic level the balance was shifting heavily in favour of the EEF. Allenby, enjoying mounting advantages in *matériel* and increasing air superiority, made exhaustive preparations for a decisive offensive intended to annihilate the Yıldırım Army Group. EEF forces were concentrated on the Plain of Sharon, where Allenby – determined he would this time not allow the enemy to withdraw intact after an initial defeat as they had after Beersheba – intended to use his infantry to break through the Ottoman front line, then unleash his cavalry to strike through the ensuing breaches to cut off the Ottoman line of retreat.

At the battle of Megiddo on 19 September, following a devastating Allied bombardment, Ottoman trenches were quickly overrun and two Ottoman infantry divisions in the Plain of Sharon effectively ceased to exist. With the Ottoman front line shattered, the Desert Mounted Corps' three divisions thrust along the coast deep into the Ottoman right flank. Early on 20 September British cavalry took Nazareth. Later that same day, the 3rd ALH Brigade took Jenin, while the 5th ALH Brigade took Samaria and, early the following morning, Nablus. Meanwhile, Allied infantry continued to advance from the south and east, rolling up any Ottoman units that tried to stand and fight. Allied cavalry swept north, capturing the coastal cities of Haifa and Acre as well as the town of Megiddo itself.

Tasked with engaging the Ottoman Fourth Army in the Jordan Valley and preventing it from intervening in support of the beleaguered Seventh and Eighth armies, the ANZAC Mounted Division pushed east from the Jordan over the Moab Mountains two days after the main offensive commenced; Es Salt was captured by the NZMR Brigade on the afternoon of 23 September, and Amman fell two days later. Also on 25 September, the 4th ALH Brigade advanced against the key rail station at the village of Semakh, on the southern shore of the Sea of Galilee, in the last great cavalry charge of World War I against a prepared position. (The 4th ALH Brigade later conducted the last brigade-sized charge of the war at Kaukab near Damascus, but this was against a disorganized rear guard, not a prepared defensive position.)

By this point, the Ottoman Eighth Army had completely disintegrated. Kemal established a rallying point at Dera for those remnants of his Seventh Army that had been able to pull back across the Jordan, sending the 3rd Cavalry Division to his right flank to block Chaytor's cavalry at Tafas. This bought enough time for Kemal to pull his units out of Dera, which was occupied by Chaytor's 4th Cavalry Division on 27 September. Meanwhile, Chauvel's Australian and New Zealand Mounted Division and the 5th Cavalry Division, racing up the coast west of Lake Tiberius, seized the key bridge at Benatı Yakup, opening up the route to Damascus. While the Ottoman 3rd Cavalry Division fought a heroic rearguard action that allowed the remnants of the Fourth and Seventh armies to pull back through Damascus, Kemal's shattered 26th and 53rd divisions as well as the 3rd Cavalry Division were trapped and forced to surrender when Allied forces took the city on 1 October. Fittingly, the first Allied detachment to enter Damascus was the 10th ALH Regiment.

Kemal pulled back to Baalbek, then to Aleppo. By this time, the battered Fourth Army had collapsed entirely, leaving Kemal's Seventh Army as the sole survivor of the three Ottoman armies that had constituted the Yıldırım Army Group on 19 September. The campaign in Syria was over, and five centuries of Ottoman hegemony over the Fertile Crescent had come to an abrupt end. The need to consolidate their gains, and the imminent onset of winter, would oblige the rampaging Allied forces to call off their pursuit for now – but Kemal faced the bleak prospect of having to organize the defence of the Turkish heartland on the Anatolian plateau itself the following year. Bowing to reality, on 30 October the Ottoman Empire negotiated the Armistice of Mudros, and formal hostilities ceased throughout the Middle East. Shortly afterwards, Germany too accepted an armistice, and World War I finally ended on 11 November 1918.

Among the repercussions of Allied victory was the ultimate extinction of the Ottoman Empire, which ceased to exist, superseded by the Republic of Turkey that Kemal, now Kemal Atatürk ('Father of the Turks'), established in 1923. Another consequence was the fragmentation of the Middle East along lines that continue to have the most profound geopolitical consequence to this day. For the ANZAC and Ottoman fighting men whose clash of arms was critical in creating this new world order, however, their war was truly over. Having converged from opposite ends of the globe to clash in battle after battle over four bloody years, they would go their separate ways once the guns fell silent, never to meet in combat again.

Refusing to accept the Allied occupation of Constantinople and the complete marginalization of a rump Turkish state, Kemal resigned from the Ottoman Army on 8 July 1919. On 4 September he assembled a national congress in Sivas, the nucleus of a nationalist parallel state that repudiated the Treaty of Sèvres in August 1920. Kemal raised a national army that defeated a Greek invasion, securing recognition of an independent Turkish republic with the Treaty of Lausanne on 24 July 1923. Having received the honorific Atatürk ('Father of the Turks') in 1934, Kemal served as president of the republic from 1923 until his death on 10 November 1938. (Keystone/Getty Images)

UNIT ORGANIZATIONS

Ottoman

In peacetime, a *Nizam* division theoretically consisted of 13 infantry battalions, one cavalry squadron, 24 field guns and supporting services, with a total strength of about 15,500 men, increasing to about 19,000 in wartime with the addition of reservists. During World War I, however, these divisions only rarely reached their establishment. Upon the outbreak of war, at least a quarter of the men flocking to the colours at the recruitment centres had to be sent home owing to chronic shortages of food, clothing and equipment. Ottoman infantry divisions had no munitions reserves or depots. At corps level, severe shortages existed in animal depots, bakery detachments, telegraph detachments and field hospitals. Only one corps had its allotted howitzer battalion, only one corps had a full-strength telegraph battalion and only one corps had its assigned cavalry regiment.

An infantry division fielded three regiments of three battalions each, each battalion of four companies; establishment battalion strength was about 700 men and 24 officers for *Nizam* battalions, 900 men and 24 officers for *Redif I* and 800 men and 24 officers for *Redif II*. Each division was also assigned a field regiment of two or three artillery battalions, each with three four-gun batteries; each three-division corps had two mountain batteries and a howitzer battalion (six-gun batteries). Each division thus maintained, on paper, between 24 and 36 field guns, typically a mixed bag of French Schneider, German Krupp and Austro-Hungarian Skoda pieces. The ammunition situation was dire; there were only about 588 shells available per gun on the outbreak of World War I. Each division also maintained a reconnaissance squadron, a machine-gun company, a pioneer company and a medical company – a total of approximately 10,000–12,000 men.

At the outbreak of World War I the Ottoman cavalry amounted to one establishment cavalry regiment and four reserve cavalry regiments assigned to the Third Army. In March 1915 the best cavalry regiments were consolidated into one cavalry division and the rest disbanded. By 1917, deficiencies in logistical capacity and the generally inferior quality of the available mounts meant there was only one Ottoman cavalry division left in action on the entire Palestine front, the 3rd, which barely escaped the trap at Beersheba.

ANZAC

In 1914, the Australian Army's infantry did not have regiments in the British sense, instead fielding battalions identified by ordinal numbers (1st–60th) derived from a specific geographical region. These regional associations remained throughout World War I and each battalion developed its own strong unit identity.

In 1914, each Australian Army division included three infantry brigades, each with four 1,000-strong infantry battalions, plus three artillery regiments, a light-horse (ALH) regiment and three companies of field engineers, for a paper total of approximately 18,000 men, 26 machine guns and 36 quick-firing artillery pieces. The smallest infantry sub-unit was the section. Two sections made up a rifle company. Each battalion had eight (from January 1915, four) rifle companies and a machine-gun section armed with two machine guns.

On 25 April 1915 the AIF had four infantry brigades with the first three making up the 1st Division. The 4th Brigade was combined with the sole New Zealand infantry brigade to form the New Zealand and Australian Division, while the 2nd Division arrived at Gallipoli in August 1915. After Gallipoli, the 3rd Division was sent directly to France and the original infantry brigades (1st–4th) were split in half to create 16 new battalions to form another four brigades of infantry (12th–15th), forming the 4th and 5th divisions.

An ALH regiment (25 officers and 400 men) was divided into three squadrons, designated A, B and C, and a squadron was divided into four troops. Each troop was divided into about ten four-man sections. In combat, three men from each section would dismount to fight on foot while the fourth man led the four horses to cover until they were needed for further action.

The New Zealand Mounted Rifles (NZMR) numbered 1,680 men, divided between the Auckland, Canterbury and Wellington mounted rifles regiments (MRR). An Otago MRR later arrived at Gallipoli as a separate stand-alone unit. Each NZMR regiment was composed of three squadrons, raised from a common geographic subdivision – Auckland, Waikato and North Auckland for the Auckland MRR; Canterbury, South Canterbury and Nelson for the Canterbury MRR; Wellington (West Coast), Wellington (East Coast) and Manawatu for the Wellington MRR; and Otago, Otago Hussars and Southland for the Otago MRR.

BIBLIOGRAPHY

Beşikçi, Mehmet (2012). *The Ottoman Mobilization of Manpower in the First World War: Between Voluntarism and Resistance*. Leiden: Brill.

Bradley, Phillip (2016). *Australian Light Horse: The Campaign in the Middle East, 1916–1918*. Sydney: Allen & Unwin.

Broadbent, Harvey (2015). *Gallipoli: The Turkish Defence: The Story from the Turkish Documents*. Carlton: The Miegunyah Press.

Bruce, A.P.C. (2003). *The Last Crusade: The Palestine Campaign in the First World War*. London: John Murray.

Cameron, David W. (2011). *The August Offensive: At ANZAC, 1915*. Canberra: Army History Unit.

Cameron, David W. (2015). *The Battle for Lone Pine: Four Days of Hell at the Heart of Gallipoli*. Melbourne: Penguin.

Cameron, David W. (2017). *The Charge: The Australian Light Horse Victory at Beersheba*. Docklands: Penguin Random House Australia.

Crawley, Rhys (2014). *Climax at Gallipoli: The Failure of the August Offensive*. Norman, OK: University of Oklahoma Press.

Daley, Paul (2017). *Beersheba Centenary Edition: A Journey Through Australia's Forgotten War*. Carlton: Melbourne University Press.

Dearberg, Neil (2017). *Desert Anzacs: The Under-Told Story of the Sinai Palestine Campaign, 1916–1918*. Carindale: Glass House Books.

Erickson, Edward J. (2001). *Ordered to Die: A History of the Ottoman Army in the First World War*. Westport, CT: Greenwood Press.

Erickson, Edward J. (2007). *Ottoman Army Effectiveness in World War I: A Comparative Study*. New York, NY: Routledge.

Falls, Cyril (2003). *Armageddon, 1918: The Final Palestinian Campaign of World War I*. Philadelphia, PA: University of Pennsylvania Press.

Fleming, Robert (2012). *The Australian Army in World War I*. Men-at-Arms 478. Oxford: Osprey Publishing.

Gariepy, Patrick (2014). *Gardens of Hell: Battles of the Gallipoli Campaign*. Lincoln, NE: University of Nebraska Press.

Grainger, John D. (2006). *The Battle for Palestine*, 1917. Woodbridge: Boydell Press.

Gürcan, Metin & Johnson, Robert (2016). *The Gallipoli Campaign: The Turkish Perspective*. London: Routledge/Taylor & Francis Group.

Hadaway, Stuart (2015). *From Gaza to Jerusalem: The First World War in the Holy Land*. Stroud: The History Press.

Harper, Glyn (2015). *Johnny Enzed: The New Zealand Soldier in the First World War, 1914–1918*. Auckland: Exisle.

Hart, Peter (2011). *Gallipoli*. New York, NY: Oxford University Press.

Kennedy, Jr., Edwin L. (2014). *The Australian Light Horse: A Study of the Evolution of Tactical and Operational Maneuver*. Auckland: PPP.

Nicolle, David (1994). *The Ottoman Army 1914–18*. Men-at-Arms 269. Oxford: Osprey Publishing.

Nicolle, David (2010). *Ottoman Infantryman 1914–18*. Warrior 145. Oxford: Osprey Publishing.

Oral, Haluk (2012). *Gallipoli 1915: Through Turkish Eyes*. Istanbul: Bahçeşehir University Press.

Ozdemir, Hikmet (2008). *The Ottoman Army, 1914–1918: Disease & Death on the Battlefield*. Salt Lake City, UT: University of Utah Press.

Perrett, Bryan (1999). *Megiddo 1918: The last great cavalry victory*. Campaign 61. Oxford: Osprey Publishing.

Perry, Roland (2015). *The Australian Light Horse*. Sydney: Hachette Australia.

Prior, Robin (2009). *Gallipoli: The End of the Myth*. New Haven, CT: Yale University Press.

Pugsley, Christopher (2016). *The ANZAC Experience: New Zealand, Australia and Empire in the First World War*. Auckland: Oratia Books.

Stack, Wayne (2011). *The New Zealand Expeditionary Force in World War I*. Men-at-Arms 473. Oxford: Osprey Publishing.

Sumner, Ian (2011). *ANZAC Infantryman 1914–15: From New Guinea to Gallipoli*. Warrior 155. Oxford: Osprey Publishing.

Weintraub, Stanley (2017). *The Recovery of Palestine, 1917: Jerusalem for Christmas*. Newcastle upon Tyne: Cambridge Scholars Publishing.

Wolf, Klaus (2020). *Victory at Gallipoli, 1915: The German–Ottoman Alliance in the First World War*. Barnsley: Pen & Sword.

INDEX

References to illustrations are shown in **bold**. References to plates are shown in bold with caption pages in brackets, e.g. **38–39**, (40).